A PRIMER
FOR CHURCH
WORSHIP

A PRIMER FOR CHURCH WORSHIP

HOYT L. HICKMAN

Abingdon Press
Nashville

A Primer for Church Worship

Copyright © 1984 by Abingdon Press

Library of Congress Cataloging in Publication Data

HICKMAN, HOYT L. (Hoyt Leon), 1927-
  A primer for church worship.
  1. Public worship. I. Title.
BV15.H52 1984   264   84-9387
           ISBN 0-687-34033-0

Portions of chapter 4 are adapted from the author's booklet *Strengthening Our Congregation's Worship*. Copyright © 1981 by Discipleship Resources.

Portions of chapter 10 are adapted from the author's leaflet *What Color This Sunday?* Copyright © 1983 by Discipleship Resources.

Scripture quotations in this publication unless otherwise noted are from the Revised Standard Version of the Bible, copyrighted 1946, 1952, © 1971, 1973 by the Division of Christian Education of the National Council of the Churches of Christ in the U.S.A., and are used by permission.

Scripture quotations noted TEV are from the Good News Bible: Today's English Version. Copyright © American Bible Society 1966, 1971, 1976.

Scripture quotations noted NIV are taken from the Holy Bible: New International Version. Copyright © 1978 by the International Bible Society. Used by permission of Zondervan Bible Publishers.

MANUFACTURED BY THE PARTHENON PRESS AT
NASHVILLE, TENNESSEE, UNITED STATES OF AMERICA

Contents

C H A P T E R

ONE

An Invitation

What was it like the last time you went to church? I don't mean just was the sermon any good or how well did the choir sing. I mean, what was it like for *you?* Did you find what you really came for? Did you know what you were really looking for?

Let's face it. Even if we're pillars of the church and are there every Sunday, sometimes we're disappointed. Have you ever said to yourself after a service, "I don't feel as if I've been to church"? If so, did you wonder whether the problem was with the service or with you?

On the other hand, sometimes we're pleasantly surprised, even astonished. Have you ever gone to church strictly out of habit, not expecting much but just doing your duty—and then suddenly, when you least expected it, felt that some kind of miracle had happened? Whether or not you could put your finger on just what it was in the service that had made the difference, maybe you came out feeling that your life was in focus, that you were right with yourself and the world and God, that you had an inner peace and power beyond anything you had expected to find.

What makes the difference? Partly it is circumstances and movings of the Spirit that are beyond our control, but partly it depends on what we ourselves bring to the service. What we put into worship affects how much we get out of it.

I hope this book will help you put more into the worship of your church. The more we hope for, look for, expect to find, the more we are likely to find. If you have ever been to church and felt, "There's got to be more than *this*," I hope you can discover what that "more" is and not be satisfied until you find it.

And you *can* find it. I don't mean that every church service has to be some kind of earth-shaking experience. There are highs and lows, and a lot that is somewhere in between. Great moments will probably be few and far between, though it helps to remember them on more ordinary days. But even when the most boring service is putting the dullest congregation to sleep, God is there, ready to break into people's lives and change them, ready to put life into that whole congregation, ready to work miracles that the people have never dreamed of.

How can you be tuned in and ready to receive what God has for you?

To begin with, you can come to church bringing an open spirit, a willingness to share yourself with the God who has a way of appearing in the most unexpected forms, and a trust that somewhere in the service God will have something good to give you.

Beyond that, it greatly helps to know what other Christians through the centuries and throughout the world have done and discovered in their worship, beginning with what the Bible says about worship and what the early Christians did when they worshiped and what worship is like today where it has been renewed and is vital. That is where this book can help.

Whenever you start questioning the way a local church worships, you are likely to hear, "But that's the way we've always done it." Tradition is very important in worship, even though tradition tends to mean "the way we did things in my home church when I was growing up," or even "the way my favorite minister taught us a few years ago." Sometimes it seems that anything done three years in a row becomes a tradition.

But if we go back to the Bible and the beginnings of Christian worship, we find that our tradition is much richer than just what our local church has always done. If we observe Christian congregations at worship around the world today, perhaps even in our own communities, we see an incredible diversity of styles. Different denominations have their diverse traditions, as do different nationalities and ethnic groups. Within a given denomination, nationality, or ethnic group, worship may range from very formal to very informal, very elaborate to very simple, very low-key to very intense. Practices such as foot-washing (John 13:1-17) and speaking in tongues (I Corinthians 12-14) are found in some Christian congregations but are totally unknown in many others. We can affirm and celebrate this diversity as God's gift.

Yet there are certain basic worship structures that have persisted through the centuries and that, even if they are not found in literally every Christian congregation, are so rooted in what our faith is about that they keep coming back even though here and there they may be rejected. These basics include the Christian calendar, the Service of the Word and Holy Communion, daily prayer and praise, and baptism. These may take radically different forms at various times and places, but they are the heart of our Christian worship.

In this book we shall center upon these four basics of worship while at the same time looking appreciatively at the diversity that exists. As we make a sort of guided tour of these basic worship structures, I shall point out some of the diverse practices that I am aware of. It would be impossible to mention every variation that exists in Christian worship. I am a United Methodist living in the United States and writing for readers who, I am assuming, will be mostly from the so-called mainline American Protestant denominations. Those whose heritage is Catholic on the one hand or more free-church on the other hand are asked to bear with what may appear to be strange inclusions and omissions. I have learned from Christians of many nationalities and ethnic groups, and I hope this shows in what follows, even as I acknowledge that my own Anglo heritage and limitations will be evident to many readers.

Now for our guided tour.

TWO

Let's Go to Church

See You in Church Sunday

If you and I are going to experience a typical worship service together, how do we do it? The answer is probably obvious. Go to church on Sunday.

But why is it obvious? Certainly we could worship God at home or on a hike or at a concert. Why go to church? And if we do go to church, why not worship there on any day of the week, at any time of day?

It's true that we can worship God anywhere, at any time, with or without other persons worshiping with us. It's marvelous to be able to feel some inner prompting and spontaneously worship God at the most unexpected times and places. If other persons are around when this happens, it's also marvelous to be able to share such an experience with them.

As good as it is to worship God spontaneously, it isn't enough in itself. We need structures and disciplines in worship as in other areas of our lives. Have you ever noticed that at those times when we have decided to worship only when we feel like it we end up worshiping less and less? When we need worship the most, we may have the hardest time getting to it. If we are not part of a worshiping congregation, worship has a way of slipping farther and farther from our consciousness. And if a group of people are to worship together as a congregation, they need to agree on a time and a place. Furthermore, when they come together, they need a common understanding of what they are to do together as their acts of worship, and in what order these acts are to come. Even if they agree to be open to the spontaneous movings of the Spirit when they are together, it would be chaos if they did not have any sort of limits or ground rules and if persons could not cue each other by means of mutually understood conventions or shared memories. A worshiping congregation typically has certain patterns and rhythms. If we are able to fall in with these, we feel "in sync," "with it." If we are not, we feel ill at ease, out of place, not at home in that worship.

All this is to say that in Christian worship time and place are important. If we are to worship together, it is not only important to be in the right place at the right time; it is also important not to be "zigging" when everybody around us is "zagging." It is important to tell a call from a response, an invocation from an invitation, day from night, Sunday from Monday, Good Friday from Easter, and (above all!) A.D. from B.C. It helps to know a sanctuary from a lecture hall, a communion table from a bargain table, and a pulpit from a conductor's podium.

One way of describing the purpose of this book is to say that it looks at the patterns by which Christians structure their time and space in order to worship together, so that you, the reader, can let these patterns bring you closer to God and to the worshipers around you.

So, if we are going to have our guided tour of worship, we need to know when and where your church has its main worship services. The answer may be "every Sunday morning at eleven in the church building on such and such a corner." Whatever the answer may be in your case, let's start with the fact that the overwhelming majority of Christian congregations worship on Sunday, usually every Sunday.

Why Sunday? Why every week? Why do we have seven-day weeks anyway? Because time—and therefore history—is important to Christians, we must often look at history to understand why we do as we do. Because the history of what God has done to make us Christians is found in the Bible, we go back especially to the Bible to understand why we do as we do. For this reason, here and elsewhere on our guided tour I will give flashbacks into history.

11

We got our seven-day week from ancient Israel, where the Jews were commanded after they had labored six days to observe every seventh day as the Sabbath, a holy day recalling how God rested on the seventh day of creation (Exodus 20:8-11, Deuteronomy 5:12-15). They referred to the days of the week as "the first day," "the second day," and so on. As other peoples in the Roman Empire and later in northern Europe adopted the seven-day week from the Jews, they named the days after heavenly bodies or gods—in English, Sunday, Mo(o)nday, and so on.

The early Christians met for worship on the first day of each week (Acts 20:7, I Corinthians 16:2), which they called "the Lord's day" (Revelation 1:10) and which we usually call Sunday. The Lord's Day was a joyous celebration, recalling that Jesus had been raised from the dead and appeared to the disciples on the first day of the week (Matthew 28, Mark 16, Luke 24, John 20). They also came to recall the first day of creation (Genesis 1:1-5); the eighth day of creation when, after resting on the seventh day (Genesis 2:2), God began to create anew; and the day of Pentecost seven weeks after Jesus' resurrection when his disciples were filled with the Holy Spirit and the Christian church was born (Acts 2).

When we worship on the Lord's Day we, like the early Christians, are saying by our action that on this "first day" we also can encounter the living Christ, can experience God's new creation, and can be filled with the Holy Spirit and renewed as the Christian church.

It is significant that we also usually worship on Sunday *morning.* Early morning was the time of day when Jesus rose from the dead and when his disciples were filled with the Holy Spirit.

To be sure, Christians since the earliest times have sometimes found it necessary or more convenient to hold their Lord's Day worship at night (Acts 20:7). Services today are sometimes held on Saturday evening, following the Jewish practice of counting days from sunset to sunset. They are also sometimes held on Sunday evening, following the ancient Roman, and modern, practice of counting days from midnight to midnight. Many Christians find that the whole

Lord's Day becomes more meaningful if they worship together both in the morning and in the evening.

Going to Church

It's Sunday, and we're getting ready to go to church. What do we do? There are various things we can do to prepare for worship, all the way from getting a good night's sleep to praying at home before we leave for church.

One thing we do is dress for church. Many people take a good deal of time and care dressing for church. Some people have "Sunday clothes" that are seldom worn on other occasions. Other people find it more meaningful to dress on Sunday as they would during the week or as they would dress for leisure activities after church on Sunday.

People have often criticized one another for the way they dress to go to church, but there are many appropriate ways of dressing for church. Someone who works at a low-status job during the week, where he or she feels like a nobody, can dress beautifully for church as a way of saying, "Here in church I am somebody." Another person who identifies with her or his weekday work can dress exactly that same way for church as a way of saying, "This is who I am, any day of the week." Still another person who must dress up every day at work may come to church dressed for leisure as a way of saying, "Here I can relax and be myself."

Not only dressing but other preparations for church may be simple or a lot of work, relaxed or hectic. Breakfast may be a set ritual every Sunday morning, complete with grace and perhaps other devotions; or the family members may be on their own to get whatever breakfast they want. There are those who live alone, families whose members can take care of their own needs, and families with children to feed and dress. Ministers and others with leadership responsibilities in church may be so preoccupied with Sunday morning preparations that their families have long since learned to leave them alone.

Whether the trip to church is a walk or a ride, it may be more than just getting there. It may be a time when exercise, or relaxation, or solitude, or togetherness helps make the spiritual transition involved in going to church.

Once we get to church there may be significant times before worship—Sunday school or visiting with friends or quietly relaxing or meditating. Some churches have a time of prayer before worship, which may be only for those such as minister and choir who will be leading worship or may be an open service which everyone is invited to attend. All such times become part of the crucial transition from being God's people scattered in the world to being God's people gathered together.

This transition isn't always easy. We come together from such different places—geographical and spiritual. Such different things may be jumbled together that need to be sorted out in our own hearts and minds. When we arrive at the place of worship and meet the other worshipers we may be rested or exhausted, calm or tense, needing to be with our friends or needing solitude, well prepared for worship or totally unprepared. It is important that we take advantage of the opportunities we have to enter into the spirit of worship and also that we be considerate of those whose needs are different from ours.

The Place Where We Meet

The physical space in which the congregation worships has more effect on both the worship and the worshiper than most of us realize. Unless worship is held outdoors, it is held in some kind of room. There is no universally accepted name for the room in which Christian congregations worship, just as there is no universally accepted name for the Sunday service held by Christian congregations. In many Protestant churches this room is called the *sanctuary*, a term which suggests that this room has been carefully designed to help the worshiper be more aware of the sanctity, the sacredness, the holiness of God.

In most churches, particularly medium-sized and larger ones, there is a sort of hallway or vestibule or lobby which is sometimes called the *narthex*. It is located between the outer door through which you enter the building and the inner door through which you enter the sanctuary. It helps us make the transition into the spirit of worship by providing a space in which people may greet and talk with each other, be welcomed by ushers or greeters or the minister, remove and hang up wraps, and be reminded by the surroundings that they are preparing to worship. On cold days it provides a place to catch one's breath after coming in out of the cold and protects those in the sanctuary from a draft of cold air every time the sanctuary doors are opened. Even in churches without a narthex you can often tell when you step directly into the sanctuary from the outdoors that there is a space immediately inside the door which serves these purposes and is not quite like the rest of the sanctuary.

Sometimes the sanctuary is reserved strictly for worship, and sometimes it is used for other purposes during the week as well. Sometimes even during the hour immediately before or after Sunday worship this room is used by a Sunday school assembly or class. Such an arrangement is not necessarily either good or bad. It may reflect the fact that the congregation has only limited space, or it may reflect a preference for an arrangement that makes worship and study and perhaps other activities feel more interconnected and unified. Wherever Sunday school is held, many persons feel it is part of their preparation for worship. Sometimes persons who have been in a Sunday school classroom find themselves entering the sanctuary not through the narthex but directly through some other door, as if to suggest that they have already had the narthex experience in Sunday school.

When you enter the sanctuary, look around the room and notice all the things that have been done to design and decorate that room for worship. Notice any assumptions that seem to have been made as to what should happen when the people worship. If there is anything about the room that seems to you to detract from worship, can you tell if this is because of someone's oversight, a lack of resources or skills, or a different idea from yours as to what worship is supposed to be?

The sanctuary is probably designed to draw your attention to some kind of worship center which is usually on a raised platform and is the focus of the worship. This worship center is likely to contain several key pieces of furniture. There is probably a pulpit, which is a stand behind or in which the minister stands to preach and from which other parts of the service may be conducted. Sometimes there is also a lectern, a smaller stand which may be used for reading and the leading of certain other parts of the service. The communion table or holy table or the Lord's table or altar is used for the Holy Communion. The baptistry or baptismal font holds water and is used for baptisms. There are seats for the choir or choirs and an organ and/or a piano in most churches. There are many ways of arranging these basic furnishings, but most American Protestant churches tend to follow one of several basic patterns.

One pattern, sometimes called pulpit-centered, was dominant during the nineteenth and early twentieth centuries and is still common. There is a raised platform with the pulpit in the center, from which the minister preaches and from which many of the other acts of worship are conducted. There is no need for a lectern. The communion table is probably in front of the pulpit on a lower level, although occasionally it is in another location or even out of sight except on occasions when communion is being celebrated. The baptistry or font can have various locations, but attention is not usually called to it unless there is a baptism. The choir may sit in a raised loft behind the pulpit or may sit on one side of the pulpit, but in either case choir members face the rest of the people. If there is a pipe organ, the casing and pipes may be prominent above and behind the pulpit. There may also be a cross above and behind the pulpit, either hanging or fastened to the wall or organ. There is a tendency to arrange the seating so that the people are as close as possible to the pulpit and choir. Thus the sanctuary may be wide, there may be no center aisle, and the seating may be curved or even semicircular.

A second pattern, sometimes called altar-centered or divided-chancel, was dominant during the middle third of the twentieth century and is still very common. In the purest examples of this type, patterned after the medieval cathedral, there are two distinct worship spaces.

The *chancel*, which is the raised area up front, may be a

large, recessed area behind an archway that is almost a
separate room, or it may be simply a platform. Against the
center of the far wall is a table, altar, or shelf that is obviously
intended to be the center of worship. A cross on or over the
altar, lighted candles on or beside the altar, and flowers in the
vicinity of the altar all suggest the presence of God through
the risen Christ. The space immediately surrounding the
altar is called the sanctuary, rather than giving that name to
the whole room. The pulpit is on one side of the chancel; and
on the other side there is usually a lectern or occasionally a
baptismal font. The choir usually sits at right angles to the
people, often in two banks on either side of the altar,
although occasionally they are seated in the rear balcony.

The rest of the people sit in the other distinct area, which is
called the *nave*. It is on a lower level than the chancel, and in
the purer examples of this type it is long and narrow, with a
center aisle. The people sit in straight rows, all facing the
chancel and the altar. Sometimes there are side areas up
front, called transepts. Seating in the transepts is at right
angles to that in the nave, but the people seated there also
face the chancel and altar. In this arrangement the people are
encouraged to focus their attention on the altar throughout
the service rather than on the minister or choir or others in the
congregation. It is important in this pattern to create distance
between the people and the altar to suggest that God, whose
presence is symbolized by the altar, is "high and lifted up." It
is appropriate for the people to relate more closely to each
other at the beginning and end of the service, however, as a
transition to and from such awesome and majestic worship,
and some feel the need of an intermission in such worship.
Not only informal greetings but also processions at the
beginning and ending of the service and at the offering serve
this purpose, since in a long, narrow nave the central aisle is
where action can be close to the people.

A third pattern, sometimes called contemporary, has
appeared in recent years. It is to date less well defined but is
characterized by a free-standing Lord's table which is central
but in more of an equal balance with the pulpit and with the
baptistry or font. The people are seated so as to be close to
these central furnishings and to one another. The worship

room as a whole is unified rather than divided into nave and chancel. The choir may be located in various places, but in any case it is obviously intended to be part of the congregation.

Once you have studied the furnishings around which the worship room is focused and which are used in the central actions of worship, look at the shell—the walls and floor and ceiling that enclose the sanctuary, define the space, and have an important effect upon worship. A long, narrow room can suggest the awesome majesty and otherness of God by putting distance between the worshiper and the center of worship, and a square or circular space can bring the people closer to the center of the action and suggest that God is in our midst. A high, vaulted ceiling likewise can suggest the majesty of God, and a low, flat ceiling can suggest God's nearness. The man who once said in my presence, "I can't worship under a flat ceiling," was saying something important about what God and worship meant to him, as are the people who tell me they feel closer to God in their little country church than in a great cathedral. Some churches are being built in the shape of a large tent in an attempt to suggest both the majesty of God and the presence of God in the midst of a close-knit people.

The composition and decoration of the shell of the sanctuary are also important. Carpeting on the floor may seem warmer than hardwood or tile or stone and, together with sound-absorbent ceilings, may also keep down the noise of conversation, although at the high cost of making the singing sound far weaker and forcing more electronic amplification. Banners, flags, and posters may appear on or near the walls. Stained-glass windows are not only symbolic and educational but also let in light of many colors. Have you ever noticed how different your sanctuary looks at different times of day? The sun may shine through an east window during a morning service and bathe the whole congregation in light, and a west window shows its full glory only in the afternoon. Evening, without sunlight but with electric light and perhaps candles, makes the sanctuary seem quite different yet. If you have seen your sanctuary only on Sunday mornings, there is probably a lot that you have missed.

THREE

What's Behind All This?

In the Bible

Now that we have taken a good look at the sanctuary, it's plain that what goes on there has a lot of history behind it. Let's suppose that we've come early enough to have plenty of time left before the service begins—time to think about how our worship came to be as it is. How did it all get started?

Sunday worship services as we know them are rooted in worship as Jesus and his earliest disciples knew it. They were devout Jews, and their worship was Jewish worship. There were the weekly synagogue services on the Sabbath and the family worship that centered around the family meal table.

We aren't sure just how and when synagogue worship originated, but it may have been in the sixth century before Christ when large numbers of Jews had been taken from their native land and found themselves in exile in Babylon. The Temple in Jerusalem, the center of their worship, had been destroyed. The Jews asked, "How shall we sing the LORD's song in a foreign land?" (Psalm 137:4). They began to hold gatherings or assemblies where there were readings from the Scriptures (what we call the Old Testament) and interpretation or teaching based on these readings. Interspersed were praises to God, probably including the Psalms. Such worship could be held anywhere that the people could gather and could be led by any man well enough educated in the Scriptures to read and interpret them. The term *synagogue,* which literally means gathering or assembly, was applied first to these assemblies for worship and later also to the houses built to accommodate these assemblies.

By the time of Jesus and his disciples, the synagogue, along with the home, was where the great majority of the Jews worshiped each week on the Sabbath. The Temple in Jerusalem had been rebuilt, but since most Jews did not live in Jerusalem and could go there only occasionally, if at all, the synagogue in the place where they lived was the center of their community worship.

Jesus began his public ministry by going around his native region of Galilee preaching and teaching in the synagogues. In his home town of Nazareth, for instance, "he went to the synagogue, as his custom was, on the sabbath day." He read Isaiah 61:1-2 from the Scriptures and then preached to those assembled (Luke 4:16 ff).

As Jesus and his disciples traveled together they also ate together, and as devout Jews they considered these meals sacred occasions to be observed with thanksgiving to God. The family meal table had long been the center of Jewish family worship. Jesus and his disciples, having left their families to travel together, had themselves become a family.

Jesus' supper with his disciples on the night before his death was both the last of these meals and the beginning of a transformed meal that Christians have eaten ever since. That night Jesus added something new to the sacred family meal they had known. As he gave them the bread he said, "This is my body. . . . Do this in remembrance of me." As he gave them the cup of wine he said, "This is my blood. . . . Do this, as often as you drink it, in remembrance of me" (Matthew 26:26 ff, Mark 14:22 ff, Luke 22:19-20, I Corinthians 11:23 ff). Actually, the word we translate "remember" might better be translated "recall" in the sense of "call back." "Do this to call me back."

When Jesus was killed his disciples were shattered and scattered, but two days later on the first Easter they found themselves face-to-face with the living, risen Christ. They found faith and meaning for their lives and a message for the world. Ever since, Christians have been an Easter people.

Luke's Gospel (chapter 24) describes the encounter of the disciples with the living Christ as worship—a transformed synagogue and a transformed holy meal. When the two disciples walking from Jerusalem to Emmaus had been joined by Jesus and had poured out their hearts to him, he quoted to them extensively from "Moses and all the prophets" (the Scriptures that Christians call the Old Testament) and *interpreted* these Scriptures to them, a term that to Luke's readers would plainly indicate what was done in the synagogue. When they got to Emmaus and sat down to their evening meal, Jesus began to do what he had done before at such meals, and "he was known to them in the breaking of the bread." Later that evening in Jerusalem, he appeared to a larger group of disciples, ate in their presence, and "opened their minds to understand the Scriptures."

John's Gospel (chapters 20–21) not only tells of the risen Christ's eating breakfast with his disciples but also tells how Thomas, when he encountered the risen Christ, said, "My Lord and my God!" Ever since, Christians have seen encounters with the risen Christ as encounters with God.

We read that Jesus then ascended into heaven, is at the right hand of God, and "fills all in all" (Acts 1:9-11, Ephesians 1:20-23). He promised his disciples, "I am with you always" (Matthew 28:20). In other words, just as God is everywhere and can be encountered and worshiped anywhere, so can the risen and ascended Christ.

Furthermore, Christ promised at his ascension, "You shall receive power when the Holy Spirit has come upon you"; this happened on the day of Pentecost (Acts 1–2). From that day to this, Christian worship has been an encounter with the living God through the risen Christ in the power of the Holy Spirit. This is one way of defining Christian worship.

After the disciples went out preaching and teaching with the power of the Spirit on the day of Pentecost, which is sometimes called the birthday of the Christian church, they continued to take part in synagogue worship wherever they went (Acts 9:2, 9:20, 13:5, 13:14 ff, 13:44 ff, 14:1, 17:1 ff, 17:10 ff, 17:17 ff, 18:4, 18:19, 18:26, 19:8, 22:19, 24:12, 26:11) and to break bread as a holy meal in their own gatherings (Acts 2:42, 2:46). Their preaching and teaching about Christ in the synagogues led eventually to a break between the Christian church and Jewish synagogues, and the Christians held their own adaptation of the synagogue service when they gathered on the first day of the week for "the breaking of bread." Such a combined service is described in Acts 20:7 ff. Interspersed with reading and preaching the Word of God, these Christians would, we gather, "sing psalms and hymns and spiritual songs with thankfulness . . . to God" (Colossians 3:16).

Through the Centuries

About A.D. 155 Justin Martyr, writing in his *First Apology* to pagans to correct vicious rumors about what Christians did when they gathered for worship, gave this description of Christian Sunday worship:

The memoirs of the apostles [that later became the New Testament] or the writings of the prophets [Old Testament] are read as long as time permits. When the reader has finished, the presider in a discourse [sermon] urges and invites [us] to the imitation of these noble things. Then we all stand up and offer prayers. . . . When we have finished the prayer, bread is brought, and wine with water, and the presider similarly sends up prayers and thanksgivings to the best of his ability, and the congregation assents, saying the Amen; the distribution and reception of the consecrated [bread and wine] by each one takes place and they are sent to the absent by deacons. (chapter 67)

Since these Christians were under persecution and had to meet secretly in homes, it is likely that services were commonly held in haste and that nonessentials were omitted. This may account for the omission of any reference to singing "psalms and hymns and spiritual songs," which would probably have been sung when possible. This may also account for the fact that the holy meal, originally a full meal, had been reduced to bread and wine, although this change may also have been a reaction to abuses such as the overeating and overdrinking by some while others went hungry, as described in I Corinthians 11:17 ff.

Christianity grew, and by the fourth century it ceased to be persecuted and became the official religion of the Roman Empire. Christians could now worship openly, build elaborate church buildings, and expand their worship services to include ceremonial entrances and glorious acts of prayer and praise. Yet Sunday worship remained at its core the synagogue service in Christian form, followed by the holy meal. To use terms more familiar today, there was the *Service of the Word* followed by *Holy Communion*.

Gradually, however, other things began to obscure the essentials, and abuses crept in. In western Europe Latin continued to be the language of worship after it had ceased to be the language of the people. Preaching declined and often disappeared, although from time to time there were outstanding attempts to renew it. There was still the Holy Communion, but it became something done by the presiding priest, far removed from the people in buildings that made the area where the clergy functioned increasingly separate from where the people were gathered. Fewer and fewer people came forward to receive the bread and wine, and a church law had to be enacted requiring Christians to receive communion at least once a year. By the fourteenth century, only priests were permitted to drink from the cup; laypersons could eat only the bread, which had become a wafer rather than full-fledged bread.

The Protestant Reformation of the sixteenth century attempted to reform many abuses in the church, including abuses in worship; but its success was only partial. The Roman Catholic Church rejected the proposed reforms and retained the allegiance of most Christians in western Europe. The Eastern Orthodox churches and the ancient oriental churches, which had long since become separated from the Roman Catholic Church in western Europe, were untouched. The Protestant churches under the leadership of Martin Luther, John Calvin, and others were successful in restoring the reading and preaching of the Scriptures in the language of the people and in restoring the people's singing of the Psalms and other forms of song. Some Protestants also restored the freedom to pray extemporaneously rather than being limited to set prayer texts.

Less successful were the attempts by the Reformation leaders to restore the fullness of Holy Communion. They did restore the right of laypersons to drink from the cup as well as eat the bread. They did restore the practice that at Holy Communion those present would partake unless there was some reason why they should not. The words used were translated into the language of the people, and there were earnest attempts to come to a more biblical understanding of the meaning of Holy Communion.

On the other hand, Holy Communion came to be celebrated only occasionally—usually quarterly or monthly—because the people, conditioned by centuries of receiving only rarely, rebelled at taking it more often. Luther and Calvin believed that Holy Communion was the natural and appropriate act to follow the Service of the Word, and Calvin left record of his deep disappointment at his inability to persuade the people at this point. They were also unable to restore to Holy Communion its original spirit of joyful celebration. It tended to penitential and even funereal.

During the next couple of centuries we see a mixed picture of renewal and deterioration in worship. Strong attempts were made to insist that at least two readings (often two whole chapters) of Scripture be read and that the sermons be interpretations of Scripture. Much congregational song was written and sung, including Psalm settings. In both Catholic and Protestant churches there was more elaborate choral and instrumental praise. Some Protestant churches managed to celebrate Holy Communion every Sunday, although popular resistance to taking communion that often eventually caused this practice largely to die out.

There were a number of especially strong renewal movements in the eighteenth century in Europe and in the eighteenth and early nineteenth centuries in America. In England, John Wesley, the founder of Methodism, placed new emphasis on reading and preaching the Word to those who were not being reached by the churches at that time, and his brother Charles wrote many popular hymns and set them to familiar and singable tunes that the people could readily pick up. The Wesleys also believed in Holy Communion as one of the key means of grace and tried, unsuccessfully, to restore its celebration each Sunday. In America there were such figures as Jonathan Edwards, Francis Asbury, Philip Otterbein, Jacob Albright, Thomas and Alexander Campbell.

All stressed the preaching of Scripture, and the Campbells were even able to establish the celebration of Holy Communion each Sunday.

In Modern America

In the nineteenth and twentieth centuries, Protestant worship in America has gone through several phases.

During the first of these, through the nineteenth and early twentieth centuries, the central concern was evangelism or church growth. When our nation won its independence, less than 10 percent of the population belonged to any church, but by the mid-twentieth century over 60 percent of the people were affiliated with some religious denomination.

At first, and in the most successful days of church growth, there was a strong emphasis on biblical preaching; but as growth slowed and preachers were trying harder and harder to make their sermons interesting to the people they wished to reach, preaching became less and less biblical. Among the Methodists, for instance, preachers in the early nineteenth century were instructed to read a chapter from the Old Testament and a chapter from the New Testament before they preached. By the latter part of the century this had changed to a *reading* from the Old Testament and a reading from the New Testament. In the early twentieth century provision was first made that a responsive reading from the Psalms could be substituted for the Old Testament reading, and later orders of worship mentioned simply a single Scripture reading and a responsive reading. Often even these were in practice omitted.

Preaching at first was based on a passage of Scripture, then upon a single verse of Scripture. This text often became a pretext for a sermon which did not really interpret the meaning of the text at all but used a key word or phrase or image to launch into an unrelated topic that appealed to the minister. It then became fashionable to begin a sermon with a life situation or illustration rather than reading or quoting a text. Sometimes a text was introduced somewhere in the middle of the sermon, but sometimes it disappeared entirely.

Congregational song, meanwhile, developed from the singing of the Psalms to the singing of hymns and songs that were saturated with biblical imagery and thought to the singing of hymns and songs that made little or no reference to Scripture.

Sanctuaries designed during this period were mostly pulpit-centered and were often called auditoriums. Where this style of worship has remained dominant, sanctuaries have tended to remain pulpit-centered.

The second phase was the "high church" or aesthetic or romantic movement that developed in England in the nineteenth century and became increasingly popular in American Protestant churches in the early and middle twentieth century. As people in the churches became more sophisticated, they became more demanding in their aesthetic taste. For many churches, the desire to *hold* people became dominant over the desire to grow. Many thought that by making services impressive—even awesome—in their beauty, people who had outgrown simpler expressions of religion would continue to find worship meaningful. There was a concern to enrich worship, to restore old traditions, to offer to God the most beautiful music and liturgies and art.

The service itself was commonly divided into two parts. The first part of the service was an increasingly elaborate and formal "morning worship," "morning prayer," or "liturgy," which included printed unison and responsive prayers and other acts of worship as well as anthems and responses by the choir. Scripture was usually read, but with little or no expectation that it was to be the basis for the preaching. In the middle of the service was a sort of intermission, consisting typically of announcements, offering, and hymn. The sermon constituted the latter part of the service. It was prefaced by little or no reading of Scripture and had little or no connection with the first part of the service. As preachers tried to hold people's attention, sermons became shorter and less biblical.

This movement romanticized the Middle Ages as the Age of Faith and the great medieval cathedrals as supreme expressions of faith. More and more Protestant churches were designed to look medieval. If that was too expensive, they at least adopted as much of the altar-centered, divided-chancel pattern as they could. This style of worship and architecture is still very common in much of American Protestantism.

A third phase, sometimes called the contemporary or experimental worship movement, was widely fashionable in the 1960s and 1970s. Here the ideal was not the great cathedral but a small group of people seated in a circle surrounded by disposable banners and posters and other artifacts made by the people themselves. Traditional forms and patterns were looked on with suspicion, and variety was valued for its own sake. Readings might be from contemporary sources as well as from Scripture; songs might be anything current (religious or secular) which reflected the people's feelings or the world they lived in; preaching tended to be a commentary on current events or a best-selling book; and there were constant attempts to find new symbolic actions such as sending up balloons or forming the congregation into a snake dance to make worship, in a key phrase of the movement, "the celebration of life." There was little interest in building new sanctuaries; existing sanctuaries were adapted or multipurpose rooms were used for this kind of worship.

These movements have all peaked and declined, although many congregations are still caught up in them and the influence of these movements is still very much with us.

Today the trend is back to basics, back to our roots, back to the Bible. We are indebted to the scholars who over the years have rediscovered the origins of Christian worship in the Bible and the early church and who have made it possible for us to recover our heritage more authentically than was possible for the church in earlier reforms. We are also indebted to the countless people in our churches who have seen or sensed over the years that we were drifting away from the Bible and from our heritage and who tried to warn those who would listen to them. We are discovering that the church today in many ways has more in common with the early church than with the established Christendom of the centuries in between.

Christians today increasingly are working to recover the

Service of the Word and Holy Communion that have been at the heart of Christian worship from the beginning. The Roman Catholic Church has made astonishing progress in this direction since its Second Vatican Council in the early 1960s. Worship is now in the language of the people. There are both a strong Liturgy (Service) of the Word and an official policy that preaching is to interpret the Scripture that has been read. At last Catholic worshipers for the most part receive communion whenever they attend and in some situations now drink from the cup as well as eat the bread. Protestant churches likewise have been realizing how largely we had let the Service of the Word deteriorate and how we have neglected the Holy Communion, and the newer worship resources have been designed to help us recover our heritage. Contemporary sanctuary designs attempt to express and support this renewed worship.

As you follow the order of worship in your local church, you are likely to see evidence of some or all of these phases of our modern American worship history. Your church may be working to renew its worship, and there may be controversy about what is being done. After this chapter on history, it is appropriate to ask what worship is and what guidelines there are by which worship can be evaluated.

FOUR

What's Happening Here?

An Encounter with the Risen Christ

Let's suppose that we are still in the sanctuary of your church waiting for the service to begin and have time to think about what is—or should be—happening when we worship.

We have seen that in the New Testament worship was an encounter with the living God through the risen Christ in the power of the Holy Spirit. Today we are in the midst of a movement of Christians to reclaim our biblical heritage and recover this kind of worship. Is there a particular story in the Bible that can help us visualize what Christian worship can be? I believe there is.

Read in Luke 24:13-35 how the disciples encountered the risen Christ on the first Easter Day, and look at going to church today in the light of that story. There is good reason to believe that Luke intended his readers to see the parallel between the events in that story and what happens when Christians gather for worship. He is saying that Jesus is risen into the life of the believer and into the common life of the believers and is promising that the reader can know the risen Christ in the service of God's Word and in the holy meal. This is one of the reasons we use the word *communion*, which translates the New Testament Greek word *koinonia*, which can also be translated "fellowship," "sharing," "participation," or "community." Christians are an Easter people, and for the Christian every Sunday is Easter Day.

That first Easter two disciples were walking together to the village of Emmaus. The risen Christ joined them, but they did not recognize him and thought of him simply as a stranger. When we come together on Sunday for worship on the journey of our lives, we too are joined by the risen Christ, whether we recognize him or not.

Jesus encouraged those disciples to pour out their hearts to him, and they did—all the defeat, disillusionment, heartache; and despair they felt now that Jesus, whom they had hoped in and believed in, had been executed. They had heard from the women the rumor that Jesus was alive, but they couldn't believe it was really true.

We too pour out our hearts in worship to the Christ in our midst and perhaps to one another as well. We may do this silently in our hearts, by joining in singing and other acts of worship, or by what we say to our family or friends as we gather. Sometimes, unlike those ancient disciples, we come in faith with joy and thanksgiving in our hearts, expecting to meet Christ. Sometimes we, like them, have sorrow and pain and defeat to acknowledge. The gospel may seem to us, as it did to them, a story that we may wish to believe but that is too good to be true. The hope of actually meeting Christ may be flickering or burned out. In any case, just as those disciples needed to share what was in their hearts before they were ready to hear Jesus interpret God's Word to them, so it is by sharing whatever experiences and feelings are in our hearts that we today become ready to hear the Word.

As Jesus quoted extensively from the Old Testament and preached on the meaning in God's plan of all the events that had so shattered the disciples, the disciples recalled later that their hearts had burned within them. In our worship today, the Scriptures are opened to us through reading and preaching and other acts of worship. It is still the risen Christ who in the power of the Spirit interprets the Scriptures. Even when Scripture is poorly read and badly preached, the risen Christ has ways of working around and through his inadequate human representatives and speaking to the worshipers. And when we respond by singing and speaking praises and affirmations, we can express the burning of our hearts.

When those travelers reached Emmaus, Jesus, whom the

disciples still did not recognize, looked as if he were going to continue on his way. The disciples had a decision to make. They could let him go, or they could invite him to stay with them. It was toward evening, and they invited him to stay with them.

We too have a decision to make when we have heard the Word. We can dismiss the risen Christ from our lives and send him on his way, or we can ask him to stay with us wherever we are, during the coming week and always. God's Word calls us to a here-and-now response.

When the two disciples, who may have been husband and wife returning to their own home in Emmaus or who may have been travelers stopping at an inn, invited Jesus to eat supper with them they naturally would have considered him their guest. What must have been their surprise when this "guest," whom they still did not recognize, started taking the role of the *host* at the table! *He* took the bread, said the blessing, broke the bread, and gave it to them—exactly as he had done three days earlier on the night before his execution. When he did these acts they recognized him, and he vanished out of their sight.

When, following the service of the Word, we share in Holy Communion, it is just as surely a communion (*koinonia*, sharing) with the risen Christ as was that supper at Emmaus. Even though we may have invited and invoked Christ's presence, it is really Christ who is the host at this holy meal and we who are the guests he has invited to participate (commune).

In their excitement the two disciples returned to Jerusalem, even though it was late, to tell the other disciples. We also can go out from worship as witnesses of the living Christ to the world.

We notice further that when these two disciples met other disciples in Jerusalem and shared with one another what they had heard and experienced, "Jesus himself stood among them." Again Jesus ate with them, and "he opened their minds to understand the Scriptures." We too, whenever we come together and share our experiences, can find the risen Christ in our midst.

The Drama of Life

When we compare the Easter story with the week-in, week-out worship of the local church, the parallel may seem impossibly idealistic, the gap too great to be bridged. How do I get from here to there—from where my experience of worship is to where it ought to be—especially if I am not in control of the worship in my church but am just sitting in a pew? How do I start where I am and find a direction to move in?

Maybe "starting where we are" means acknowledging that many of us now tend to see worship as a sort of performance, as if the minister and choir were actors and chorus on stage and we were the audience, watching and listening, criticizing the performance—if not aloud at the time, then at least over the Sunday dinner table. We hear the minister talk *about* God and Jesus, but it may never occur to us that God through Christ is actually taking part in what is going on.

But if we want to think of worship as a drama, it is a far greater drama than that. The stage is not just the chancel or platform up front. The whole sanctuary is the stage, as Søren Kierkegaard told us over a century ago (*Purity of Heart*, Part XII), and the members of the congregation are actors. The minister is the director as well as being one of the actors. God is both the Audience and the Playwright. The script is the Scriptures, and the play is the drama of life.

We can think of worship services as the rehearsal of life. Like other rehearsals, they should not be too cut-and-dried for learning to take place. The minister, as director, has studied the script, interprets it, adapts to the situation in which the drama is taking place (life here and now), and works to bring the actors and the action together into a coherent whole. But remember, the Playwright is present and has the right to interpret the script. The Playwright doesn't have to sit back passively beyond the footlights. The Playwright may walk on stage and mingle with the actors. The Playwright may whisper to the director, who in turn can relay the word to the other actors; but the Playwright is equally free to speak directly to any of the actors. After a service the actors scatter better prepared to take their various roles in the performance of the drama of life all through the week.

But worship services are more than rehearsals; they are life itself as it should be lived. Like rehearsals, they prepare us for the Christian performance of life during the rest of the week. On the other hand, they do not take place simply for the sake of what happens during the rest of the week; they are the crucial part of the performance itself which serves as model for all the rest. When we are gathered together in our services of worship, we relate as Christians to God and to other people; and when we are scattered in the world, we are to do the same. If Christian worship means relating in a Christian manner to God and to other people, then all life should be worship. This is the ideal which our services of worship model.

What would happen to you if you took this understanding seriously? What would happen to your local church if even a few persons dared to take this understanding of worship seriously? Do you dare to believe that your life is part of a vast drama and that your part is important in the eyes of the Playwright, even though you may not grasp the whole plot and even though your local congregation may be only a tiny fraction of the entire cast? Are you studying the script at home and listening attentively as it is interpreted by the director? Are you sensitive to the other actors, relating your role to theirs and learning from them? Are you alert to hear whatever the Playwright may be saying to you? Are you learning so that in the coming week you will play your part well in the drama of life?

Worship Is Central

Certainly such an understanding of worship makes clear that worship is central to the church as a whole, to your local church, and to your participation in the church.

In worship the people of your congregation discover and are reminded that they *are* the church. In the worship of the church we are reminded of who we are and what, by God's grace, we are becoming. Important as it is to ask and plan what your local church is *doing* as the church, the most basic thing is *being* the church. You can leave out any other part of the program of your local church, important as it may be, and still have a church if you have regular worship. But if you don't have congregational worship you don't have a church.

The living Christ who promised, "I am with you always," does for the congregation at worship, week in and week out, what he did for those first scattered disciples—but with this one basic difference: *now* it is possible for us to come joyfully *expecting* an encounter with the risen Christ and focusing our attention on the fact of his presence. He reveals himself to us in the power of the Holy Spirit. He bonds us to himself and to each other anew as his people, his family, his Body. He enables the Body to grow, gives to each member of the Body the gifts that are needed in the role to which each is called, and empowers the church as an institution for its corporate witness in the world.

It is no wonder that in most local churches more people are present for Sunday worship than at any other time and for any other purpose during the week. Even if there are other occasions when as many people attend as on Sunday morning—an evangelistic service, a church school assembly, some other special service—these are almost always worship services, or at least occasions when worship is an important part of what takes place.

Often in the long history of the worldwide church, congregations have flourished with only one scheduled activity each week—Sunday worship—during which children, youth, and adults of every age were trained and educated, counseled and advised, nurtured and supported, and equipped for action during the week. Today a great many churches of small membership carry on an effective ministry with no regular weekly meetings except congregational worship and perhaps a church school which itself includes worship.

Imagine the church forced to cut back its program to the absolute minimum, as in times of persecution. There have been, and still are, times and places where congregations as we think of them have not been permitted, where they could gather only as families and small groups in secret. When they managed to come together in such circumstances, what was their chief, and often their only, corporate activity? Worship.

Even in a large congregation with a seven-day-a-week program, corporate worship is central. To be sure, persons in such congregations often feel more sense of belonging to a church school class, an organization, or a small group within the congregation than to the congregation as a whole. But these smaller groups commonly worship in their meetings; and the main congregational services of worship remain the central act by which a large and diverse congregation is, and feels itself to be, one local church rather than many.

It is in congregational worship, therefore, that a local church is most open to change and growth. Nothing will permeate the whole life of a congregation with the felt presence and power of God as deeply and extensively as the coming to life of its worship. While spiritual renewal can originate in a local church elsewhere than in its Sunday worship, that renewal will either bring new life to congregational worship or be severely limited, if not stifled, by the continuing deadness of that worship.

Worship is crucial in winning persons to Christ and his church. When persons first visit your local church, they probably come with questions on their minds that make their first impression of your worship crucial to their whole future relationship with your church and perhaps to their Christian faith. Whether they are newcomers to your community who have had an active church relationship somewhere else or persons who have been invited to your church and heard good things about it or persons who have come on impulse because your church was handy and looked inviting, they have come because they are looking for something.

As they take part in the singing and prayers, hear the Scriptures and sermon, relate to the members of your congregation, read and listen to announcements of what your church is doing, they will be forming impressions that help them answer the questions on their minds. Is this the kind of church I am looking for? What does it stand for? Is there anything here that meets my needs? Are these people that I would like to be associated with? Could I become enthusiastic about what this church is doing? If they decide to join your church, what they have experienced in its worship will probably have been a very important part of the reason.

Persons who commit themselves to Christ and join the church need to be part of a supportive worshiping community if they are to be nurtured and grow in the faith. Even if they are familiar with the basic gospel message, they need to be reminded of it regularly. They need a fuller knowledge of the story and teachings of the Bible. They need to participate in public prayer and learn from the example of other Christians how to pray and praise God in any setting, public or private. They experience in their interaction with other members of the Body a model of how Christians love one another and act out the gospel. In this community they can meet members of the Body with differing gifts and perspectives and, by broadening their horizons, become better grounded and more mature Christians. And if this is true for others, isn't it also true for you?

Basic Principles of Worship

This whole understanding of worship suggests certain basic principles which can help us know what to want and what to look for in worship.

1. *Worship should be biblical.* The Scriptures are our script and should be opened to the people through reading, preaching, and other arts and media. Prayer and praise have a particular power when they use words of Scripture. Over a period of time a congregation should be exposed to a full and balanced coverage of the whole Bible.

2. *Congregational participation is crucial.* This includes not only unison and responsive acts of worship, spoken and sung, but also participation by laypersons in the planning, leadership, and evaluation of worship. It also means that laypersons, as well as ministers, have particular gifts which are appropriately offered as part of worship.

3. *Worship should be inclusive.* It should include our bodies as well as our minds, our emotions as well as our thoughts, every one of our senses. It should include children, youth, and adults of all ages. It should include women and men. It

should include every racial, ethnic, and cultural heritage represented in the congregation. It should include persons with handcapping conditions. It should include persons not just as passive observers but as active participants.

4. *Spontaneity should have a place.* If the Playwright is to interpret the script, if worship is an encounter with the living God through the risen Christ in the power of the Holy Spirit, then no matter how carefully planned the worship is, there is always the possibility, even the likelihood, that the Spirit will lead someone to do the unexpected. That someone does not have to be a minister but can be a layperson.

5. *Order should also have a place.* Persons feel freest to follow the Spirit if they have a basic sense of pattern and structure within which there is freedom and from which one may occasionally depart. Both rigidity on the one hand and chaos on the other make most people withdraw into their shells.

The Order of Worship

We saw in chapter 3 that there is a historic order to the Service of the Word and Holy Communion, but that this order has been subject to wide variation.

What sort of order does Sunday worship have in your church? When you walk into a worship service in your church, you are probably given a leaflet containing the printed order or program of the service that day. This may be called the bulletin. Sometimes the service is read out of a book instead or proceeds by announcement or follows a pattern that the worshipers know by heart or is more or less spontaneous.

In any event, the worship in your church probably follows a basic pattern week after week. Within that pattern there may be more or less flexibility, and on special occasions the usual pattern may not be followed at all. Most of the time, however, the regular worshiper has a good idea what will come next, even without looking at a printed order of worship. A church may go through a stage in its history when it is ready for a trusted minister or other leaders to take it through a period of experimentation, but even then it usually is not long before a pattern emerges.

The worship books and orders of worship of many Christian denominations have been revised in recent years to restore the ancient patterns of the Service of the Word and Holy Communion, sometimes referred to today as the Service of Word and Table. One denomination, The United Methodist Church, describes this pattern as follows *(General Services 1984):*

The Entrance
The people come together in the Lord's name. There may be greetings, music and song, prayer and praise.

Proclamation and Response
The Scriptures are opened to the people through reading of lessons, preaching, witnessing, music, or other arts and media. Interspersed may be psalms, anthems, and hymns. Responses to God's Word include acts of commitment and faith with offerings of concerns, prayers, gifts, and service for the world and for one another.

Thanksgiving and Communion
In services with Communion, the actions of Jesus in the Upper Room are reenacted:

> taking the bread and cup,
> giving thanks over the bread and cup,
> breaking the bread, and
> giving the bread and cup.

In services without Communion, thanks are given for God's mighty acts in Jesus Christ.

Sending Forth
The people are sent into ministry with the Lord's blessing.

You may wish to examine the pattern of worship in the Sunday services of your local church. Do you find the historic Word-and-Table pattern there? Has it been modified? If so, how? Do your worship services follow an entirely different pattern? If so, you might try to find out where it came from and why it was developed.

Meanwhile, let's continue to suppose that we are in the sanctuary of your church as the people are gathering for a

Sunday service. The descriptions in the next chapters may or may not fit the worship of your church in every detail, but I hope that they will help you understand better what is happening when your congregation worships and what can happen for you when you worship.

FIVE

The Service Begins

When Does the Service Begin?

Suppose we have been sitting quietly in the church sanctuary for a while, absorbed in our own thoughts. At first, no one else was in sight. Now people are beginning to gather. The minister and the choir are not yet in place, and no music is being played. We might wonder, "When does the service begin?"

The bulletin, the bulletin board outside the church, the ad in Saturday's paper, and the newsletter you got through the mail all agree that the service is at 11:00—or whatever your advertised hour may be. But that's not as simple as it sounds. "The service is at 11:00" can mean different things in different churches. And because time is important in Christian worship, we can more easily worship in a congregation if we can get "in sync" with its kind of time.

Church A thinks it knows exactly what 11:00 means. At 10:30 or 10:40 the first worshipers enter the sanctuary; at 10:50 the organist enters and plays a prelude; at 11:00 sharp the organist sounds eleven on the chimes (you can set your watch then!), and immediately one hears the words of a call to worship or the opening notes of a processional hymn. Anyone arriving at 11:05 or 11:10 is quietly smuggled into a seat by an usher who acts as if such lateness is an embarrassment that calls for a cover-up.

Church B goes by a different kind of time. An 11:00 service means that the first worshipers do not usually enter until a few minutes before the hour. At about 11:00 (it doesn't have to be at the exact minute), the organist enters and begins the prelude, and it is five or ten minutes after the hour when the first words are spoken or sung. At least twice after that there are momentary pauses in the service, at points duly noted in the bulletin, for something regarded as a normal part of the order of worship—the seating of latecomers.

Church C goes by still another kind of time. An 11:00 service means that somewhere around that time the first worshipers appear, but don't worry if you arrive at 11:00 and find yourself the first one there. A little later, as soon as enough people have gathered, the organist begins to play. A little later, when most of the people have arrived, come the opening words and hymn. Worshipers continue to arrive after that, and no one worries about lateness.

We could easily describe more patterns, but the point is that each congregation worships by its own kind of time and has developed its own set of expectations. These are probably no problem to the regular worshiper who knows what to expect, but they may be a problem to a visitor who is accustomed to a different kind of time. Visitors from Church C arriving at 11:15 to worship in Church A may feel embarrassed, and visitors from Church A arriving at 10:55 to worship in Church C may have the panicky feeling that they have gotten the time of service wrong. We can hope that someone will be on hand in both situations to help these visitors feel warmly welcomed and comfortable.

When does the service begin? We saw in chapter 3 that from the beginning Christian worship services have been "gatherings." The word *congregation* is derived from a verb meaning "to flock together." The New Testament word we translate "church" means "assembly." Some Christians refer to worship as "meeting" or "having church." If we take this understanding seriously, then the service begins whenever people start to gather for worship.

The Gathering

While the service as a whole is a *gathering*, the term is sometimes used to refer particularly to the first part of the service when the people are literally in the process of gathering. What actually happens to begin the worship in your church as the people are gathering? Congregations differ widely, but several customs are common. (1) Sometimes a church bell or bells or amplified music sounds from the church tower through the neighborhood to call people to worship. (2) As the people come together there are informal greetings, conversation, and fellowship. (3) There may be a period of informal singing. (4) Announcements may be made and visitors welcomed. (5) Occasionally there may be rehearsal of music or of other acts of worship which are new to the people. (6) Organ or other instrumental music may be played in the sanctuary to encourage quiet meditation, reflection, or prayer.

These customs are often combined in various patterns. For instance, (2) may be encouraged inside the sanctuary before (6) begins and thereafter only outside the sanctuary. (3), (4), or (5) may either precede or follow (6).

None of these customs or patterns in itself is better or worse than the others, but in a particular local church or on a particular occasion one of these customs or patterns may be far more appropriate than another. Some congregations find it best to follow the same pattern every Sunday, while other congregations prefer to vary the pattern.

Persons have diverse needs as they gather for worship, and this fact can cause problems. The organist is playing; some persons want to be reflective and meditative; other persons want to greet and catch up with friends they haven't seen for a week or more. It is easy to suggest that those who wish to talk can do so outside the sanctuary while those who wish music and reflection can be left undisturbed in the sanctuary, but this is not as easy a solution as it may sound. Whatever pattern is customary in your church, you may often be called upon to exercise patience and understanding with some of your fellow worshipers while at the same time expressing your own needs.

More is happening while the people gather than meets the eye. We believe that God is present through the risen Christ in the power of the Holy Spirit. Present, too, is the whole Body of Christ, the whole people of God, the whole church.

We who gather here this Sunday are not simply two or three or thirty or three hundred members of one local church, who live in the same community, are affiliated with the same denomination, and are "our kind of people" (whatever that means). We are also "a great multitude that no one could count, from every nation, tribe, people and language, standing before the throne and in front of the Lamb. . . . wearing white robes, . . . [crying] out in a loud voice: 'Salvation belongs to our God who sits on the throne, and to the Lamb [Christ]!' " (Revelation 7:9-10 NIV). If the seating arrangement in your sanctuary is slightly curved, as if part of a much larger seating going around your pulpit and table, it may suggest to you that the few people visibly present in your church today are only a small part of a much larger circle, the family of Christ, which neither distance nor denominational barriers nor death can break. Our gathering includes the whole communion of saints—those who have ever lived, those who live in the world today, and generations yet unborn who will praise God's name.

There are special moments when the leaders of worship enter the gathering. The organist or other instrumentalists may be the first of these to enter. The pastor may be present informally greeting people throughout the gathering, or may quietly at some point during the gathering take his or her place up front, or may enter as part of a procession. The choir or choirs, too, may enter quietly and inconspicuously or as a procession while singing. There may be such other persons as an associate pastor, a song leader, or a layperson who is assisting in the leadership of the service. One or two acolytes may enter and light candles either in the midst of the gathering or as part of a procession.

Some or all of these persons may be wearing robes or vestments which signify their special function in worship and which remind us of the invisible multitude which is the larger part of our gathering. An academic robe, sometimes worn with a hood, signifies the educational preparation and teaching ministry of the minister. An alb, or light-colored robe adapted from the basic garment worn by men and women alike in the early days of Christianity, is a link with what was worn by the early Christians, reminds persons of the biblical "white robes," and can symbolize the presence of the whole communion of saints. Albs may properly be worn by laypersons as well as by ordained ministers. The stole (colored scarf) worn around the neck and hanging down in front over an alb or academic robe, on the other hand, has from ancient times signified that the wearer is ordained.

A Variety of Gifts

As we see these worship leaders taking their places, let's take a look at their roles. Paul tells us (I Corinthians 12) that there are varieties of gifts and varieties of service in the Body of Christ. For us, as for the Christians in Paul's day, it is as hard as it is vital to appreciate this variety of gifts in congregational worship.

Let's start with the ordained minister. As was mentioned earlier, the minister is both the director of worship and also one of the worshipers. The minister is sometimes spokesperson for God to the people, as when reading Scripture and preaching, and sometimes spokesperson for the people to God, as when leading prayer. This does not mean that ordained ministers are the *only* persons through whom God can speak to the people or the people pray to God. God can speak to any and all of us, and we all can pray to God.

What distinctive gifts, then, does the ordained minister bring to worship; and what does ordination authorize a minister to do in worship? While different denominations understand ordination differently, and while you may wish to discuss with your pastor how she or he understands ordination, it is usually understood to include at least three authorizations in relation to worship: (1) to preach the Word (interpret the Scriptures); (2) to officiate at baptisms, Holy Communion, weddings, and funerals; and (3) to order the worship of the congregation within whatever are the prescribed guidelines. Ordination is generally understood to certify that the minister (1) has been called by God to this particular ministry; (2) has the faith, commitment, and gifts required for this ministry; and (3) has undergone the necessary studies and other preparation so that he or she knows how to carry out this particular ministry. The church, through a process that usually involves a local congregation and then the wider denomination, examines candidates for ordination, certifies its satisfaction that they are called and qualified, and ordains them with the invocation of the Holy Spirit. The ordained minister is commonly understood to be in some sense the authorized representative of the wider church and its heritage in the local congregation at worship so that this worship may be more fully the worship of the whole communion of saints.

Today more and more laypersons are taking leadership roles in worship such as reading Scripture, leading prayers and other acts of worship, expressing prayer concerns, and making announcements. This is in keeping with ancient Christian customs and has brought new life to many congregations.

Choir directors, choir members, and those who play musical instruments bring special gifts to worship—their calling and commitment to the ministry of music, their talents, their training and education, their experience in the leadership of music and worship. This is true of the ready and willing persons with little or no training who offer the best that they have to give, just as it is true of the professional musicians who offer *their* best.

Actually, the whole congregation acts as the choir in the singing of hymns, songs, choruses, and responses and as a speaking choir in unison prayers and in other unison and responsive acts of worship. This is part of what was meant by the statement that the members of the whole congregation are actors in worship. The congregation usually has one or more smaller ensembles (choirs) and instrumentalists who (1) give leadership to the congregation's acts of worship, (2) act as spokespersons for the whole congregation to God, and (3) act as spokespersons for God to the congregation. Let's look at these roles in more detail.

1. A good choir continually leads the rest of the congregation in worship. If choir members are seated where the rest of the congregation can see them, they can cue the congregation when to stand up and sit down and can use body language to be an effective example of attentive

worship. By their leadership, the choir and the instrumentalists can greatly strengthen congregational singing, particularly if a congregation is learning something new.

2. Some acts of worship—anthems, for instance—require rehearsal for which the congregation as a whole cannot be expected to give time, and often demand special abilities and training which most persons in the congregation do not have. Listeners can identify with such acts of worship and feel that the choir and instrumentalists are being their spokespersons to God. Much music today helps congregations do this by including parts for the congregation as well as for soloists or choir.

3. God speaks powerfully to people through music. Scriptures are often "opened" and Christian witness is often given most effectively when set to music. This music is often of such character that it must be sung or played by an individual or a small group rather than by the whole congregation.

There are also special gifts brought to worship by ushers and greeters. Their leadership is especially important during the gathering time at the beginning of worship, during the offering, and during communion.

Sometimes worship is enriched by gifts of drama, sacred dance, clown ministries, and related arts.

Persons often provide or arrange flowers, altar cloths, banners, and other visuals.

We remember the custodian or whoever cleans and prepares the sanctuary for services, the secretary or whoever produces the bulletin, the acolytes and those who train them, and all the other persons in the church who have some assigned role in the services.

When we add to all these gifts those that come from rank-and-file members of the congregation we have a wide (and possibly wild!) diversity that is rewarding and perhaps hard to live with. We can think of each minister or musician who comes along, "Why isn't he or she like so-and-so?" and wonder why we're always disappointed; or we can ask, "What gifts does this person have for us?" and help him or her to grow in the exercise of these gifts. The fussy baby, those who are moved to praise the Lord in the most unexpected time and way, the critic who mumbles a complaining commentary on the service, and the monotone who makes more noise than a dozen people singing in tune are in the same service with the perfectionists who feel their worship has been spoiled if the slightest thing goes wrong, the short-fused who shoot a glare or a frown in the direction of anyone who is the slightest bit conspicuous, and the kids of any age who are looking for the slightest excuse to chuckle or snicker. There is no way that you or I can make the rest of the congregation behave our way, but if we add our gifts to theirs we can all go away enriched by what has taken place.

C H A P T E R
SIX

Prayer and Praise

The Greetings

The first major turning point in the worship service comes when the minister, choir, or other leaders of worship start speaking or singing in such a way that the attention of the whole congregation is focused on the presence of God in the gathered congregation and on the dialogue taking place between God and the congregation. There is commonly such a major change in the focus of the congregation at this point that people are likely to assume that it is the beginning of the service, although as we have seen, the service is already well under way.

This turning point can take various forms. The minister may call the people to worship God, and the people may respond by greeting God with a hymn of praise. Sometimes the first words are a hymn of praise to God, during which the minister and choir may enter in a procession and after which the minister greets the people and calls them to some further response such as prayer. Sometimes the choir sings a call (or *introit*), which leads to a response in which the people greet God with prayer or praise. The minister may begin by invoking the Trinity or by reading or quoting a sentence of Scripture in which God is calling to the people, and the people respond with prayer or praise to God.

These patterns are all greetings—both people-to-people and also between the gathered people and God. As such, they all involve call and response. An understanding of call-and-response patterns is basic to an understanding of our worship.

Worship is a dialogue, a conversation, a sharing, an exchange, a communion between God and the gathered congregation and also from person to person. It is a very special kind of dialogue, as these opening greetings illustrate. The minister or choir greets the people not simply as one person to another, but *in the name of God and of the risen Christ.* It is acknowledged that God has initiated the dialogue and is acting through whoever is speaking or singing the greeting. The people respond not simply to the person or persons who address them but to God.

This special dialogue is typically carried on in a special language. When we address God, or speak in God's name, it somehow doesn't seem right to talk exactly as we would in ordinary conversation. On the other hand, we want to be ourselves and speak from our hearts. Sometimes language styles in worship swing back and forth as we try to find the right way of expressing ourselves in God's presence.

Many of us grew up hearing a very special kind of language in church, either because it was printed that way in a ritual or because the ministers and devout laypeople used that language when they prayed and conducted services. God was addressed as "thee" and "thou." Strange words like *shouldst* and *wouldst* and *beseech* kept coming in. Words like *seek* and *redeem* and *grace* were used more often than in ordinary conversation and with different meanings. The whole style seemed old-fashioned and stilted. It was explained to us that because God was so holy, we should show respect by using this special style with God. Some carry this distinction further and pray or worship in another language entirely.

Many of us also react against this style, especially if we have had experiences that have made God or Jesus seem more like our dearest friend than like an authority figure. Not only is God addressed "you," but a conversational, even chatty, style is used as it would be with a friend. Every effort is made to steer clear of "stained-glass language." If slang can be used, so much the better.

But stained glass has its purposes, in windows and in

language. We don't feel quite right about being chummy with the Almighty, and a group of people gathered for worship is not the same as a group of people chatting at a party. Somehow it doesn't seem quite possible consistently to talk with God exactly as we would with anyone else. A chatty style can be just as much of a mask as a formal style. Dignified and respectful language can be just as natural and honest as slang.

So where does this leave us? Is there a middle-of-the-road worship language that is both natural and reverent? You may have noticed these language shifts in your church, and you will doubtless have your own feelings as to what is most appropriate. You may wish to share these feelings with your pastor sometime.

The dialogue of worship is carried on with more than words and music. We have already seen that in churches the worshipers are surrounded with visual symbolism, with messages for the eyes. The physical sensation of standing or kneeling or bowing our heads helps us be more alert and sensitive to God's communications *to us* as well as more wholly expressive in our prayer and praise *to God*. As we continue to study our worship, we shall discover that all of our senses are channels of communion with God and with each other in Christian worship.

And as we are aware of what is going on in our inward being, we can be more alert to those promptings and insights which come to us through no outward senses but which are channels for God's presence and guidance. "Be still and know that I am God." The God who is closer than our breathing is nearer than we think.

Acts of Prayer and Praise

After the opening greetings there are commonly acts of congregational prayer and praise. These may constitute an elaborate prayer-and-praise service, sometimes called morning prayer or morning worship, which takes the first half of the service and is followed, after an intermission of announcements and offering, by the reading and preaching of the Word. It may be simply an opening hymn of praise and a prayer, leading immediately into the reading and preaching of the Word. It may be a more or less extended song service. There may be one long all-purpose prayer or scattered shorter and more specialized prayers. Whatever the pattern in your local church, let's take a look at what happens in this time of prayer and praise.

Prayer is a response to God's call and is part of an ongoing call-and-response pattern that characterizes all our worship. The call, given in the Lord's name, may be simply, "Let us pray." It may be a longer sentence, or an exchange between minister and people, or something sung by the choir. The prayer itself which is in response to this call may be led by a single person or by several persons in turn, or it may alternate between leader and people (a form sometimes called a *litany*), or it may be prayed in unison. Whoever is leading the prayer is praying on behalf of the whole congregation, and indeed we are being joined in prayer by the whole communion of saints. Sometimes a prayer is an alternation of calls to prayer and prayers, sometimes called a *bidding prayer*. All these prayers may be spoken, or they may be sung. A very large proportion of our hymns, choruses, and anthems are prayers. A soloist singing a prayer is just as surely leading prayer as is the minister who speaks a pastoral prayer.

When the congregation is being led in prayer, it is traditional for the people to affirm the prayer by responding "amen"—which means in Hebrew "so be it" or "I agree." When the people say or sing "amen" at the end of a prayer, it means that they agree with the prayer and are making it their own. It is much more appropriate that this "amen" be said or sung by the whole congregation rather than by the minister or choir alone. Even if your congregation is not used to saying this "amen" out loud, you can quietly say it yourself. More and more persons have been doing this in recent years, and in many congregations this practice has gradually caught on until "amens" are heard all over the congregation and finally acknowledged as something the congregation does. In many congregations the people say "amen" or "praise the Lord" or "yes, Lord" or similar words at any point in a prayer when they feel moved to do so. Sometimes this is done very quietly, if there is reason to fear that other worshipers may not appreciate such interjections; but in other congregations it is accepted and done out loud.

A congregation prays by means other than speech. We can pray silently, and times of silent prayer are part of many worship services. Many Quakers worship in total silence, except as persons may be moved to speak or sing; and if a Quaker meeting on a given day is entirely silent, this is considered perfectly appropriate. Through sacred dance or interpretive movement, one person, a few persons, or a whole congregation may pray in body language, either in silence or while words of prayer are being spoken or sung. Congregations of the deaf conduct worship in sign language, and in many other congregations someone signs what is said or sung—that is, interprets it in sign language, both for hearing-impaired persons present and also because many persons who can hear the words find that the signing adds another dimension to their prayer.

In any public prayer the congregation expresses its participation by some form of body language. In biblical times and in the ancient church the posture for prayer was to stand, and this is often the posture for prayer in churches today. (Cf. I Samuel 1:26, Matthew 6:5, Mark 11:25, Luke 18:11.) Sometimes the leader, and perhaps other persons as well, adds the biblical raising of somewhat outstretched hands, especially if the prayer is one of praise or thanksgiving. (Cf. I Kings 8:22, Psalms 28:2, 63:4, 134:2, 141:2, Isaiah 1:15, Lamentations 2:19, 3:41, I Timothy 2:8.) Other persons and congregations kneel, especially if the prayer is one of confession. Still others remain seated, perhaps bowing their heads and making a special effort to sit straight and alert. Some persons pray most naturally with their eyes closed, others with their eyes open. The point is not that one posture is correct and the others wrong; it is that persons and congregations are free to decide what a given posture says to and for them as they pray to God.

There are different kinds of prayer. *Praise* is adoration and thanksgiving for God's own goodness and power. It overlaps with *thanksgiving*, which may be praise or may be giving thanks for the gifts God has given us. *Petition* or supplication is asking God to act on our behalf. Two special forms of petition are *invocation,* where we ask for the gifts of God's presence among us, and *confession,* where we acknowledge our sin and unworthiness and ask for God's forgiveness. *Intercession* is asking God to act on behalf of someone else.

In some services all these kinds of prayer are combined into one long prayer, which some call the *pastoral prayer.* In other services there are several different prayers for different purposes. Many churches find that if there is only one prayer it tends to be mostly petitions and intercessions, with little thanksgiving and praise and even less confession. For this reason there is often a special prayer of confession, introduced by a call to confession and followed by a time of silence for personal reflection and then a declaration of pardon by the minister which may quote words of assurance from the Bible.

Many churches make provision in their prayers of petition, intercession, and thanksgiving for persons to express their prayer concerns. This may be done in various ways. In congregations and rooms small enough that anyone can speak and be heard by everyone, persons may be invited to pray spontaneously in turn, expressing whatever concerns may be theirs. Such prayers should be kept very brief, so as to give others a chance without unduly prolonging the prayer. In average-sized churches persons may be invited to express their prayer requests or concerns. The congregation may pray a response such as "Lord, hear our prayer" after each concern; or the minister or other leader may gather up these requests and concerns into one prayer. In other congregations, especially if they are large, persons either make the pastor aware of their concerns ahead of the service—perhaps through cards dropped into a prayer request box placed where people can use it on their way into the service—or use cards placed in their seats and pass them forward with the aid of the ushers. The minister then uses these cards in forming the prayers of petition, intercession, and thanksgiving. Sometimes, whatever way is used, there is a special time or effort to elicit joys and thanksgivings, since otherwise the concerns may be largely sorrows and petitions.

There are some special prayers and praises that are widely

said or sung in unison every Sunday and which people who attend church are likely to have memorized.

The chief of these is the Lord's Prayer, which was taught by Jesus to his disciples and is found twice in the New Testament (Matthew 6:9-13 and Luke 11:2-4). It contains in its few words every one of the above kinds of prayer. It is the supreme Christian prayer and the summary of all Christian prayer, and most churches include it in every Sunday service. It can easily and appropriately be sung by the congregation to one of the many available musical settings. As we shall see below, it has a particularly traditional and appropriate place immediately before the serving of the communion bread and wine.

The Doxology is also widely sung. The term *doxology* refers to any prayer of praise to the Trinity, and many of our hymns contain a doxology as their final stanza. The one many Protestants refer to as the Doxology was written by Thomas Ken (1637–1711).

> Praise God, from whom all blessings flow;
> Praise him, all creatures here below;
> Praise him above, ye heavenly host;
> Praise Father, Son, and Holy Ghost.

This is usually sung to the tune "Old 100th," which was originally written for the paraphrase of Psalm 100 entitled "All People That on Earth Do Dwell." The Doxology is sung today to several other tunes, with several variations of the wording.

Also commonly sung is the Gloria Patri, which is Latin for "Glory to the Father." The words date from the third and fourth centuries and are rooted in numerous phrases in the Bible itself. It has been sung to many different musical settings since that time, most commonly as a New Testament or trinitarian ending after the singing or reading of one of the Psalms. There are now two commonly used English translations:

> Glory be to the Father
> and to the Son and to the Holy Ghost;
> As it was in the beginning,
> is now, and ever shall be, world without end. Amen.

Glory to the Father,
and to the Son, and to the Holy Spirit:
as it was in the beginning,
is now, and will be forever. Amen.

Proclamation and Response

God's Word

After the opening prayer and praise comes the main part of the Service of the Word, which may be called proclamation and response. This is the time when God's Word is proclaimed to the people and when the people make appropriate responses to the Word.

The move from prayer and praise to proclamation and response is a dramatic turning point in the service. Up to this point the emphasis has been on our prayer and praise to God. Now the emphasis will be on God's Word for us and our response. It is like that moment on the walk to Emmaus when the two disciples had finished pouring out their hearts and Jesus began quoting and interpreting the Scriptures to them (Luke 24:25-27).

This turning point is often marked by a brief prayer in which we pray that the Holy Spirit may enlighten and empower the reading, preaching, hearing, and doing of God's Word. Such a prayer is often prayed by the minister, but in some ways it is even more appropriate that a layperson lead this prayer. If the opening section of prayer and praise is short, this invocation is often included in the opening prayer.

What do we mean by *God's Word?* It is a term that is used in three closely related senses: God's Word written (Scripture), God's Word preached (the sermon), and God's living Word (Jesus Christ). The reading and preaching of the Word are means by which the living Word (Christ) speaks to us.

The Scriptures need to be "opened" to the people—that is, set before the people in such a way that their message is made plain and Christ can speak through them. Traditionally and most commonly this is done by reading one or more passages of Scripture and then preaching on part or all of the Scriptures that have been read, but there are other ways in which this can be done. Scripture can sometimes be sung, dramatized by two or more persons, visualized through film or other media, enhanced by sacred dance or interpretive movement, or witnessed to by persons who tell of their own experience.

Sometimes these ways of opening the Scriptures make a subsequent sermon unnecessary. The singing of a cantata that tells the story of Jesus' passion or the acting out of the passion narrative from one of the gospels, for instance, might well take the place of a sermon.

But since reading and preaching the Scriptures are how we usually hear the Word proclaimed, let's look at this pattern more closely.

Reading the Scriptures

Since ancient times the reading of Scripture has involved call and response.

There is a sense in which this is continually going on as Scripture is read and preached. The people respond inwardly and let their responses show in their body language—the expressions on their faces, their posture, spontaneous nods and shakes of their heads. In many congregations it is customary to punctuate the preaching with responses like "amen," or "praise God," or "preach"—sometimes so constantly that the antiphonal call-and-response rhythm is apparent.

There has been since ancient times another, slower call-and-response rhythm as the reading of Scripture is interspersed with acts of praise such as psalms, anthems, hymns, or other responses. These acts of praise may be sung or spoken—in unison by the congregation, antiphonally between leader and people, between different parts of the congregation, or by choir or soloists. In any case, this is done on behalf of the whole congregation to express the people's response of praise to God for the message of God's Word. Also, each reading may begin or end with a set form of words which embodies a call and response. Thus, at the end of a reading the reader may say, "This is the Word of the Lord," and the people may respond, "Thanks be to God." Or the reader may say (his or her personal response of) "amen," after which the people may say "amen."

In a growing number of congregations one or more of the Scripture lessons are read by a layperson rather than by the pastor. This follows ancient custom and is one of the ways laypersons can easily and effectively share in the leadership of worship. By their careful preparation of the reading and by their sense of the importance of the ministry they are performing, readers of Scripture can make readings among the high points of the service. It is both fair to all segments of the congregation and also more interesting and effective if the readers chosen over a period of time represent, in fair proportions, women and men, youth and young adults as well as middle-aged and older adults, and whatever ethnic and cultural variety is in the congregation.

The reading of Scripture is seen as well as heard, and there are ways of making it visually effective. At the beginning of the service, or just before the Scriptures are to be read, the Bible which is to be read from may be ceremonially carried to the pulpit or lectern, either processionally down the aisle or from wherever the Bible may have been during the week. In other churches the Bible sits open on the pulpit or lectern at all times as a symbol of the function of the pulpit as the place from which God's Word is read and preached—opened—to the people. The Bible used is commonly a large and impressive "pulpit Bible." Its size and imposing appearance signify the importance of Scripture in our worship, and its print is large enough to be easily read.

A layperson who reads Scripture often sits in the midst of the people until time for the reading, then comes forward. This is a way of involving the congregation more closely in the reading and of not separating the reader from family or from the rest of the people.

The Rhythm of Proclamation and Response

Proclamation and response can occur in various patterns. These usually have a call-and-response rhythm, although this is more obvious and extensive in some orders of worship than in others. Compare these three patterns.

In Church A the preacher reads or quotes from memory a short verse or so of Scripture, which is the text for the sermon, and then preaches the sermon itself. This is followed by a hymn in which the people express their response and during which persons sometimes come forward to join the church or for other acts of commitment.

In Church B there is this pattern:
Scripture reading
Hymn
Scripture or text to be preached
Sermon, ending with prayer or invitation
Creed or other acts of commitment

In Church C there is still another pattern:
First Scripture
Psalter
Second Scripture
Hymn or sung response
Gospel
Sermon, ending with prayer or invitation
Creed or other acts of commitment
Concerns and prayers of the people

Each of these churches has its own rhythm of proclamation and response, but there are important differences. Notice especially how they differ in the amount and variety of Scripture read and in the variety of responses used.

The Growing Place of Scripture in Worship

There has been a growing tendency in recent years to read more Scripture. At least two passages, and often three, are read in an increasing proportion of churches at each Sunday service. This recovers traditional practice and is especially helpful today when the only Scripture a great many persons ever see or hear is what is read in the Sunday service. When two or three readings are used, it is not necessary that the preacher deal with all of them in the sermon. God's Word can be communicated by an act of reading done well.

There has been a related trend toward systematically covering the story and message of the Bible over a period of time in a given congregation. If this is not done, it is easy for the preacher to "ride hobby horses" and repeatedly read and preach from certain favorite passages.

The most commonly used system of covering the basics of Scripture is the *lectionary*, a three-year cycle of suggested Scripture readings which was developed in the late 1960s and early 1970s by scholars of many denominations and is now used throughout the world by churches of numerous denominations. This lectionary offers several advantages. Pastors have discovered that it does a far better job of covering the story and teachings of the Bible than any plan they could devise, particularly given the busy schedules of pastors today. A large number of helps for planning worship and preparing sermons are now issued in dated form to follow the lectionary, and in many communities two or more clergy get together each week to share insights and ideas regarding the Scriptures in the following Sunday's lectionary. In many churches the Scripture readings are distributed to the congregation in advance for private reading, for weekly Bible study groups, and for the benefit of musicians and others who have a part in planning and preparing services.

Of course, use of the lectionary is not an all-or-nothing matter. Some pastors see the lectionary as their starting point and then feel free to substitute other Scriptures as circumstances in the life of the congregation may warrant. Still other pastors systematically preach through the Bible by a plan which they themselves have devised. You might ask your pastor, if you do not already know, what plan she or he uses for covering the story and teachings of the Bible.

Another recent trend has been the recovery of the Psalms as the most basic and traditional hymnal or collection of acts of praise that Christians have. The acts of praise—psalter, anthems, hymns, and other responses—that intersperse our worship have always taken their words more from the Bible, and especially from the Psalms, than from any other source. Today, after years in which the use of Scripture in Christian praise declined, our Christian songs are again increasingly based on Scripture, especially on the Psalms. It might be interesting for you to investigate how many of the anthems and hymns that your church uses take their words from the Bible. Most hymnals list the biblical sources or references of the hymns they contain.

Psalms are used in worship in many ways. Since the lectionary includes a psalm as part of the recommended Scriptures each Sunday in the three-year cycle, many pastors and musicians are finding some way each Sunday to use the lectionary psalm. In many Protestant churches psalms are read responsively by leader and people, or by two sides of the congregation. These "responsive readings" are included in many hymnals. Increasingly churches are discovering, however, that psalms are more effective as acts of praise when sung. Many hymns and anthems are psalm paraphrases. Other musical settings of psalms involve an easily learned—or already familiar—refrain or chorus (traditionally called an *antiphon*), sung by the people in response to verses of the psalm spoken or sung by a leader. Still other congregations or choirs chant psalms in unison or harmony.

The Sermon

Regardless of your church's particular pattern of proclamation and response, the reading of Scripture and related acts of praise lead to the sermon and to the response called for by the sermon.

In most Protestant worship the sermon occupies the central place. The average Protestant minister probably receives more training in sermon preparation and delivery than in any other phase of worship planning and leadership. He or she probably spends more time each week in sermon preparation than in all other forms of worship preparation combined.

As you listen to the preaching, it helps to have in mind some basic questions. What is the preacher trying to do?

What does the preacher want to happen in your life as a result? What do *you* want to happen? Most important, what is *God's Word* saying to you?

Preacher A, for instance, is trying to make points and may even feel it is important that there be three points in each sermon. This preacher is trying to communicate a series of abstract teachings in such a way that you will believe them and act on them. She or he prepares a sermon by first thinking of a topic, then dividing it into points, and then searching for illustrations which will clarify each point and make it easier to remember. These illustrations may be taken from the Bible, from personal experience, or from what the preacher has read or heard from others. But these illustrations are there to support preconceived points and to deal with a topic already chosen.

Preacher B, on the other hand, may be trying to produce a total emotional effect rather than communicate detailed content. The stories told, the phrases used, and the manner of delivery are all designed to produce some feeling such as joy or comfort or guilt. The structure of the sermon is not a series of points but the building up of this feeling.

Preacher C follows still a different purpose and preaches a sermon that *is* a story, normally a Bible story or a story that illuminates the writing of some particular Bible passage. The sermon moves from scene to scene rather than from point to point, and there is no attempt to tack a point on to the story. The preacher wants the hearer to remember the story itself and be changed by it.

You also may have your expectations, and these may be either fulfilled or disappointed. You may hope for help in dealing with a particular life situation, and the sermon this Sunday may or may not speak to your situation. You may be expecting a sermon to have one point (or three points) that you take home and remember all week. Your pastor may not preach a point-making sermon but may be like Preacher B or Preacher C. If your pastor is like Preacher A, you may find that you remember an illustration but forget the point, that you take a while to tune in to the preacher and miss the opening sentences, or that you are not constantly paying attention during the sermon but are "in and out" and hear only snatches of it. If so, you are perfectly normal.

The fact that it is much easier for most persons to remember a story than a series of points is one reason that more and more sermons today are stories. Such a style also fits well with preaching from the lectionary or any other plan that aims to familiarize the people with the basic story in the Bible.

As you listen to a sermon, the ultimate question is not what *the preacher* wants, or what *you* want, but what *God* wants you to hear and do. You may hear something which the preacher wasn't aware of and didn't intend, but which can be God's Word to you and which can change your life. Even if your mind has been wandering, suddenly you may hear something which gives you an insight that is God's gift to you—though this may be far from what the preacher had in mind. Especially when the preacher is faithfully reading and preaching the Bible, there is much more in preaching than even the preacher is aware of.

What Do You Do After the Sermon?

Preaching is a call in search of a response. Whether or not there is a formal invitation to Christian discipleship at the end of the sermon, a sermon itself ought to be an invitation to Christian commitment.

The ultimate response to God's Word is the character of our Christian faith and life day by day, but an immediate response is also important. If we simply walk out of church after the sermon without doing anything to affirm our *commitment* to what has been proclaimed—our *ownership* of the Word—then we have missed an opportunity to do something that would strengthen us as we go back to be Christians in our weekday world.

Ministers often end their sermons with the call, "Let us pray," after which they lead the congregation in a prayer which expresses the hoped-for response. Ideally, each person makes this prayer his or her own act of commitment and signifies this by adding a personal "amen." The danger is that this prayer will be experienced as simply an extension of the sermon and a solo act of the minister.

A stronger response is a hymn following the sermon, in which the congregation expresses its commitment and faith. This hymn may be chosen because it expresses a response appropriate to the sermon just preached, or it may be a general hymn of praise or thanksgiving.

In many churches there is an invitation to Christian discipleship following the sermon and before what may be called the invitation hymn. During this hymn, the words of which may express both call and response, persons may come forward to profess or reaffirm their faith in Christ, to be baptized or present children for baptism, to be confirmed, or to join the church by transfer.

Sometimes the invitation is expressed more broadly so that persons may also respond with acts such as giving a personal witness, making some response to the sermon, or making a commitment to a particular form of Christian service or a particular course of action.

There may be a period of silent reflection, sometimes with the understanding that persons are free to break the silence as they may be moved to speak, pray, or sing.

Many churches use a creed or affirmation of faith as a congregational response to the Word. While a creed can occur at various points in the service, it is especially appropriate as a response to the Word because it is an expression of our commitment and faith. The Apostles' Creed and the Nicene Creed, both of which date from the early Christian church, are the ones most commonly used. The Apostles' Creed, which originated in the early church as a profession of faith for those presenting themselves for baptism, is appropriate not only at baptisms but on any Sunday as a reminder of the faith into which we have been baptized.

Increasingly the period of concerns and prayers is placed after the sermon as a response to the Word. This follows the pattern described by Justin Martyr in the second century and enables us to make more specific our commitment to God and to the needs of our neighbors.

Sometimes the character of the service makes a congregational prayer of confession followed by a declaration of pardon an appropriate response.

The offering of money and gifts for the work of the church or for the needy is often placed after the sermon as a response to the Word, a symbol of our larger offering of ourselves and all that we have in God's service. The offering can be received at various points in the service, and its placement helps to determine its significance as an act of worship. Sometimes it functions primarily as an intermission. Even if it is in the early or middle part of the service, however, it may be intended to symbolize our commitment in response to what has preceded it. A key symbolic moment in many offering ceremonies occurs when the ushers, who have received the offering from the people, bring it forward and place it—or give it to the minister to place—on the Lord's table as prayer or praise is spoken or sung.

Immediately before the offering, the people in many churches exchange with each other words and gestures of God's peace. This is particularly effective if a prayer of confession and declaration of pardon have just taken place. Reference may be made to Matthew 5:23-24: "If you are offering your gift at the altar, and there remember that your brother has something against you, leave your gift there before the altar and go; first be reconciled with your brother, and then come and offer your gift." Exchanging the peace is mentioned in Romans 16:16, I Corinthians 16:20, II Corinthians 13:12, I Thessalonians 5:26, and I Peter 5:14. It is more than simply greetings all around. It signifies that we are at peace with our neighbors in the spirit of Christ and that we love and forgive one another as God through Christ has loved and forgiven us. For this reason the exchange of peace is also sometimes placed following the Lord's Prayer.

The peace and the offering are commonly a bridge between the Service of the Word, where they function as response, and Holy Communion, for which they are preparation. It is fitting that we turn now to Holy Communion.

C H A P T E R

EIGHT

Thanksgiving and Communion

The Basic Pattern

We have already seen that in the historic pattern of Christian Sunday worship the Service of the Word is followed by Holy Communion. This holy meal is also called the *Lord's Supper* (I Corinthians 11:20), the *Breaking of Bread* (Acts 2:42), and the *Eucharist* (from the New Testament Greek word for thanksgiving). These terms may be used for the whole service, including the Service of the Word. Here we shall use the term that is perhaps most familiar to Protestants—*Holy Communion*—and use it in its narrower sense to refer to the service of the table or holy meal which follows the Service of the Word.

For most Christians and during most of church history, Holy Communion has been inseparable from the Service of the Word. The two together have formed the main Sunday service of the church.

For the majority of Protestants today, however, it is only an occasional service—perhaps monthly, sometimes only quarterly, sometimes on certain high occasions in the church year, sometimes weekly but at a time other than the main Sunday service. It is often either a more formal ritual tacked on to the usual—and less formal—Service of the Word or it is from beginning to end a whole different order of worship from that followed on other Sundays. In either case it is experienced as less familiar and comfortable than the Service of the Word. The services of Holy Communion printed in our hymnals and

66

other worship books sometimes have so many printed prayers and other words to be read that we get the impression that Holy Communion is primarily a complicated ritual of words.

Fortunately, this is beginning to change. We are recovering the basic biblical simplicity of the holy meal. Both Protestant and Catholic churches have been reforming their practice at the Lord's table, and you may have noticed in your local church how Holy Communion has changed in recent years.

The Bible makes clear what we have so often forgotten in the past—that this holy meal is a *meal*. It is eating bread and drinking wine with the living, risen Jesus Christ and with our sisters and brothers in Christ at Christ's own table. The living Christ is hosting us just as surely as when he ate with those first disciples while he preached and healed in Galilee and Judea, when he ate with them on the night before he gave his life for us, and when he was recognized by the disciples in those first resurrection meals.

We have seen that since the earliest years of the Christian church this holy meal has usually been a token meal of bread and wine rather than a full-course meal, but this does not change the fact that it is a meal. Our everyday lives are full of token meals that fulfill the communal purposes of eating and drinking together on occasions when we neither need nor want to eat a full-course meal. When we visit a friend or attend a party or take a break at work, we consider token eating and drinking perfectly natural even if it isn't mealtime and we aren't especially hungry.

Increasingly we are making Holy Communion more clearly a meal. The Lord's table is designed to look and function like a meal table. A loaf of real bread is used instead of special wafers or pellets that neither look nor taste like bread. Our style of eating and drinking at the Lord's table is designed to feel like real eating and drinking together, even though it will always feel like a very special kind of eating and drinking together.

Because it is a meal, Holy Communion is basically a series of actions in which words, while essential, are less prominent. As we look at the New Testament meals that are our models for Holy Communion, we find four simple actions. Following Jesus' own actions, we in his name (1) take the bread and cup, (2) give thanks over the bread and cup, (3) break the bread, and (4) give the bread and cup to each other. (Cf. Matthew 26:26-28, Mark 14:22-23, Luke 22:17-20 and 24:30, and I Corinthians 11:23-25.) While speaking may take place during any of these steps it is only the second step, giving thanks, that is primarily a matter of words. Since the first and third of these actions are very brief and preliminary to the second and fourth, we might see the steps as two: (1) taking the bread and cup and giving thanks over them, and (2) breaking the bread and giving the bread and cup to one another. These two steps may be referred to simply as thanksgiving and communion.

Churches have different ways of doing these acts and different policies as to who is authorized to do them, but the general pattern is clear.

First the presiding minister or elder takes the bread and cup and gives thanks over them. The bread and wine may be brought forward by designated persons, who may be those who have prepared them if they are homemade, as they often are. Or they may be brought from some nearby table to the Lord's table. Or they may already be on the Lord's table and be uncovered at this time. The minister or elder then makes any necessary preparation of the bread and wine. The bread may be leavened or unleavened, the wine fermented or unfermented. The use of a single uncut loaf of bread is symbolically powerful and is growing. It has an even stronger biblical basis (I Corinthians 10:16-17) and seems to arouse less objection than the use of a common cup, although that practice is also being restored in many churches.

Just as we give thanks or say a blessing over our food and drink when it is brought to the table at home, so we do at the Lord's table. This blessing, sometimes called the Great Thanksgiving or the Eucharistic (Thanksgiving) Prayer, is led by the presiding minister or elder, and there are usually responses by the people. This crucially important prayer expresses in words what we are doing when we celebrate Holy Communion. The minister or elder traditionally gives thanks to God appropriate to the occasion, remembering God's acts of salvation through Jesus Christ and the institution of Holy Communion by Christ himself. In some traditions the minister or elder also prays that what we offer to God may be joined with Christ's offering for us, invokes the power of the Holy Spirit, and makes intercessions. The prayer traditionally ends with a doxology (praise to the Trinity) and a great amen sung or said by the people.

The minister or elder in ancient times stood behind the Lord's table to preside and at appropriate times during the Great Thanksgiving adopted the biblical gesture of raised and outstretched hands. This posture, discarded through the centuries by many churches, is today increasingly regarded as symbolically the most effective and is being widely restored.

Following the Great Thanksgiving it is traditional to pray the Lord's Prayer as a bridge between the thanksgiving and the communion, and in some churches this is followed by the exchange of the peace.

The communion includes breaking the bread and giving the bread and cup. The minister or elder continues to preside but is often assisted by others in the distribution of the bread and wine.

The ancient practice of first breaking by hand the uncut loaf is being restored in many churches. This may be done in silence or may be accompanied by appropriate words. It is powerfully symbolic of Paul's words in I Corinthians 10:16-17, which is the passage on which our use of the terms *communion* and *Holy Communion* is based. Our partaking of the one loaf signifies that we are one body. The bread which we break is a *koinonia* (communion, participation, sharing, fellowship) in the body of Christ, and the cup over which we give thanks is a *koinonia* in the blood of Christ. Sometimes the cup is also raised as a gesture of invitation to partake.

The bread and wine may be distributed in various ways. The people may come forward and receive standing, seated, or kneeling. The bread and wine may be passed while the people remain in their seats or with the people standing in a circle if it is a small congregation. This is the climax of the whole service, the act that unites us to the living Christ and to the whole communion of saints in heaven and on earth. This act constitutes, or reconstitutes, us as the Body of Christ, the universal church. Often during the communion the people sing hymns, gospel songs, and choruses which express the intimacy and joy of our union with Christ and one another. This is a good time to sing the most familiar and beloved songs, preferably ones that the people know by heart or can readily pick up by rote without having to use a hymnal.

What follows the communion is usually brief, a reentry into a more ordinary plane of life. The Lord's table is set in order. There is usually a brief prayer of thanksgiving after communion, a hymn may be sung (Matthew 26:30, Mark 4:26), and the people are sent into the world with a blessing *(benediction)*. The communion bread and wine may be taken afterward to the sick and others unable to attend. Some reverent disposition is made of the remaining bread and wine.

Some churches take care that Sunday services when Holy Communion is omitted include either thanksgiving for God's mighty acts in Jesus Christ or at least recitation of these mighty acts in one of the traditional creeds.

The Meanings of Holy Communion

What does it all mean? Thousands of books have been written through the centuries and throughout the world on the many meanings of Holy Communion. If what this act means could be put into words, then the act itself might be unnecessary and we could content ourselves with the words. Words can only point in the direction of what has to be conveyed by the experience itself, and even the experience grows and changes as we do. One facet of meaning will be most important to one person, another facet to another person.

The fact that this act is called by a variety of names suggests that each name adds some facet of meaning. "Holy Communion" shows the holiness and intimacy of the union with Christ and his Body which it creates and expresses. "Lord's Supper" shows that it is a meal hosted by our Lord. "Eucharist" shows the spirit of thanksgiving which permeates it. "Sacrament," from the Latin term for a soldier's pledge of allegiance, shows that it is our pledge of commitment to Christ and his church. "Ordinance" shows that it has been instituted and ordained for us by Christ.

All kinds of statements, each true as far as it goes, can be made about the symbolism of the bread and wine and what we do with them.

Breaking the bread and pouring out the wine represent the breaking of Jesus' body and the pouring out of his blood on the cross—and more! They represent the giving and pouring out of his total life and ministry—his birth, life and teaching, suffering and death, resurrection and ascension, presence today, and final victory. The offering of the bread and cup to everyone present proclaims Jesus' offering of himself for us and for everyone.

The dividing and sharing of the bread and wine demonstrate our stewardship not only of the gospel but of all God's gifts, including the fruits and resources of the earth. They are to be shared with all people, even as we share the bread and wine with the whole congregation.

Receiving the bread and cup from the hand of another person represents our receiving God's love in Christ, which comes to us through other persons. Giving and receiving food have always been primary ways in which the human race has given and received love. As we taste and see the bread and wine, we remember the words of the psalmist (34:8): "Taste and see that the LORD is good."

Sharing the one loaf of bread and remembering Jesus' words, "This is my body," are indeed a participation *(koinonia)* in the one Body of Christ.

Remembering Jesus' words, "This is my blood, which seals God's covenant" (Matthew 26:28 TEV), and drinking from the cup do indeed renew our covenant relationship with God, sealed once and for all by the shedding of Christ's blood.

Moreover, this "cup of blessing" represents life. The Old Testament repeatedly identifies blood with life (Genesis 9:4, Leviticus 17:11, Deuteronomy 12:23). By sharing this cup we participate in the life of the risen Christ. The wine we receive renews the life of Christ in us.

Holy Communion not only gathers together the past and present, it anticipates the future. We eat and drink this "until he comes" in final victory (I Corinthians 11:26). This token of food and drink is not only a foretaste of heaven for each of us, it is also a foretaste of the messianic banquet when Christ shall have have won his ultimate victory.

We could go on indefinitely with such interpretations. Each is a perspective from which we can see part of the whole meaning of Holy Communion. Those who find one perspective most helpful do not have to argue with, much less separate from, those who find another perspective most helpful. Christians have argued and fought over just *how* Christ is present, *how* the bread and wine are changed, *how* the service should be conducted, *who* is authorized to preside at it, and *who* is eligible to receive the bread and wine. Surely this family meal of Jesus' disciples should bring us together in love, not keep us apart!

Ultimately, the Holy Communion which we have with God in Jesus Christ is a mystery. The New Testament speaks of "the mystery of the gospel" (Ephesians 6:19), "the mystery of the faith" (I Timothy 3:9), "the mystery of our religion" (I Timothy 3:16), "the mystery of Christ" (Colossians 4:3), "this mystery, which is Christ in you, the hope of glory" (Colossians 1:27), "the mystery of God" (Revelation 10:7). We are "stewards of the mysteries of God" (I Corinthians 4:1). When a minister or elder presides at this holy meal, no matter how much theological education and spiritual maturity he or she may have, this sacred responsibility that has been entrusted to him or her is that of a steward who passes on something that goes beyond the understanding of any of us. God may reveal to you in Holy Communion something that the minister did not intend or was not aware of, and that's all right. None of us is so wise as to have plumbed the depths of the mystery.

On the other hand, the mystery of the gospel is revealed even to young children—perhaps *especially* to young children, if we remember Jesus' words (Mark 10:13-16). Baptism, as we shall consider below, is initiation into the mystery of Christ. Those churches that baptize infants, that consider them ready for initiation into the mystery, are increasingly admitting them to Christ's family meal as well. A small child who eats and drinks at this holy meal already knows the difference between being accepted and rejected at a meal table and already connects being fed with being loved. Through this holy meal God can reveal the mystery of the gospel to children at whatever their stage of development.

In fact, as we get older our theories and explanations sometimes get in the way of God's revealing the mystery to us. If somewhere in the process of growing up you learned some neat formula to explain Holy Communion, you may not realize that your understanding did not begin with that formula and will not end with it. On the other hand, if you have difficulty participating in Holy Communion—or even stay away—because it doesn't make sense to you or because some interpretation you have heard is incredible or offensive, perhaps the interpretation you once heard should be put aside in favor of one more suited to your present stage of maturity or in favor of more openness to the mystery.

Many persons have stayed away from communion over the years because they misinterpreted Paul's warning: "Whoever, therefore, eats the bread or drinks the cup of the Lord in an unworthy manner will be guilty of profaning the body and blood of the Lord. . . . For anyone who eats and drinks without discerning the body eats and drinks judgment upon himself" (I Corinthians 11:27, 29). If we read the whole passage (verses 17-34), we discover that Paul was referring to a situation in the church at Corinth (in Greece) where persons were bringing their own food and drink and sometimes eating and drinking to excess while refusing to share with those who had brought nothing and were going hungry. Those selfish persons were obviously communing in an unworthy manner. They failed to discern the Body of Christ—the hungry people right there in front of them who were members of Christ's Body. They were shutting themselves off from the Christ who was in "the least of these" (Matthew 25:31-46).

Paul's warning has nothing to do with the level on which we can intellectually understand the theology of Holy Communion. If we can be glad for the blessing which Christ gives not only to children but also to the mentally retarded and the senile at the holy table, we can be glad that

Christ's invitation includes us, regardless of our level of understanding.

Paul's warning also has nothing to do with our present level of moral development, provided we come willing to let Christ raise us from wherever we are, whether we are the worst sinner or the greatest saint, to something higher. Receiving communion in a worthy manner is not at all the same as taking communion because we think we are worthy. The only way any of us is worthy is through God's gift in Christ, and to come to the Lord's table because we thought we had earned the right to be there would in itself be an unworthy motive. Christ has always been known as one who liked to eat with sinners (Luke 15:2), and he still does.

So come to the table and let Christ feed you food to grow on.

NINE

Day by Day

Back into Daily Life

Whether or not there has been Holy Communion, the service usually ends with acts that send us out into the everyday world.

There is usually a dismissal with a blessing in the name of the Trinity, given by the minister and often called the *benediction*. In its traditional form it is *not* a prayer; it is spoken to the people face-to-face. It is therefore appropriate to keep your eyes open and look at the minister, since she or he is talking to you.

A closing hymn, sometimes with a recession by minister(s) and choir, may express and strengthen our sense that we are going as Christians into the world.

A postlude may be played in a spirit of joyous praise. In some churches the people remain seated and listen, while in other churches the music accompanies the people's going out.

People may stand around and talk for a while, either in or immediately outside the church building, before scattering. Others may wish to leave quickly and quietly.

All these acts are part of the worship service and, like what has gone before, help give worship its crucial place in the drama of life. During the week the persons who are "on stage" with us will have attended rehearsals other than the one in our local church, or no rehearsal at all. God the Playwright will still be present, but we shall need to be perceptive if we are to keep in touch.

Constant communion with God, and feeling the constant

support of other Christians when we are not face-to-face, is a sublime ideal. It can become increasingly a fact as we grow in the Christian faith and life. It becomes possible to perceive God's leading in all kinds of events day by day. More and more we can find ourselves spontaneously praying exclamations, phrases, sentences silently—perhaps even out loud— to the God who is always with us. We can internalize Scripture so that passages come to mind when needed. What we sing in church can come to our hearts if not our lips as our song whenever the Spirit moves. All meals can be a holy mystery, and even when we eat alone we can know the presence of the communion of saints.

But let's face it, most of us are a long way from this ideal. If we are to move in this direction it needs to be step by step, and this means structure—a structure of time and perhaps a structure of place as well. Some persons need more structure than others. We all need some mixture of structure and freedom.

We have already noticed how *time* is important in Christian life and worship. The structure of the week is important. The internal structure and rhythm of the worship service are important. The structure of the day is important—to our life and to our worship.

Most of us have some kind of daily cycle and structure. Unlike the cycle of the week or the rhythm of a service of worship, the cycle of day and night is given in nature. Unless we are in the Arctic or Antarctic, there is a structure of day and night every twenty-four hours. If you have ever spent a long time in a windowless room or underground, you know how disorienting it can be not to experience day and night.

The *time* of day is also important. Most people structure their days around such times as getting up and going to bed, going to and from work or school, mealtimes, break times, times to have fun, times for favorite television shows.

Daily Worship

What has all this got to do with worship? A great deal. If our relationship to Christ and his family is to make any

76

difference day by day and not be something we forget about from Sunday to Sunday, we need some pattern of daily worship. The traditions of daily worship that have persisted among Christians through the centuries have taken advantage of existing structures. There are long and rich traditions of morning and evening prayer, both in the form of personal and family devotions and for larger gatherings. Sometimes there are both evening prayer at the end of the working day and night prayer before sleep. Even the heritage in monasteries of prayer at three-hour intervals, which seems incredibly removed from life as most of us know it, is strikingly parallel to what many of us experience as the common daily rituals of breakfast, midmorning break, lunch, midafternoon break, dinner, and bedtime.

Structures of place and support systems of people may also help you through the week. If your church means a great deal to you, it may help you to return to church for services or meetings between Sunday mornings. There may be a special place at home or at work where you find it easier to reflect and get in touch. You may belong to a small group that meets regularly, includes such forms of worship as Bible study and prayer, shares faith and experiences with one another, and may have some sort of agreement as to personal daily Bible reading and prayer. You may engage in Bible reading, prayer, singing, or other devotional practices as a family.

Since this book is about public worship, this is not the place to enter into a discussion of personal, family, and small-group worship. These are of central importance in themselves, and other books deal with them. What is important to note here is that daily worship, even if not usually done in a congregational setting, both is nurtured by Sunday worship services and in turn becomes the foundation upon which Sunday worship is supported and grows.

Another way in which we are nurtured in our daily worship is by the model of daily worship we experience when we are at a church conference of almost any sort, particularly one which extends over at least one night. Such conferences, camps, retreats—whatever they may be called—commonly mark the turning points of the day by some form of worship. There is probably a morning service when singing and prayers take note of the fact that another day has begun. At the end of the afternoon or at the end of the evening or at both times, there is probably a service when prayer and praise remind us that the sun has set and evening or night has come. Lesser turning points in the day may be marked by a hymn or a brief prayer.

Some congregations are situated where they can offer brief morning, noon, or evening services for persons on their way to or from work or during lunch hour. Some schools, particularly theological seminaries, have daily services and may, in addition, open class sessions with prayer. Such services commonly contain references to the time of day.

In churches where this is not feasible every day it is often done on Sunday and perhaps once in the middle of the week. Morning prayer and the singing of morning hymns are often features of the first part of Sunday morning worship, or there may be a short prayer service before the main Sunday service. Sunday evening services are important in many congregations and take advantage of the fact that in the evening most persons are more open and expressive, particularly at the level of their feelings, than they are earlier in the day. Evening hymns such as "Day Is Dying in the West" and "Now the Day Is Over" may be sung. Midweek morning and evening services are likely to take on the character of the time of day in which they are held.

Such services may provide models which help us structure our daily personal or family worship. Giving thanks (blessing) and perhaps other acts of worship at meals can remind us of the sacredness of all eating together and can be an occasion to note the turning of the time of day, and a time to remember family and others who are not physically present. Many persons set aside a quiet time—when they first get up, before they begin the day's work, at some "break" time such as the lunch hour, at the end of work, or at the end of the evening. This may be the briefest moment, or it may be longer if possible. Some persons who find themselves waking in the middle of the night find it helpful to mark these times with a momentary prayer. One family remembers fondly its tradition of Sunday evening family hymn sings. Another family treasures what members can do on their vacations that is not possible at home. Still another marks family reunions at times such as Thanksgiving and Christmas with ritual acts of various sorts.

If there is a special need today in family worship, it may be to recover more use of Scripture. Daily worship at its best includes some plan—and there are many good plans—for reading through the Bible. The Psalms in particular have been at the heart of daily worship throughout Christian history, and the historic traditions of Christian daily worship make extensive use of the Psalms every day. In fact, if there is one great secret to bringing daily prayer to life, it is knowing and using the Psalms and making their incredibly open and honest style of prayer and praise your own.

TEN

The Christian Year

The Rhythm of the Year

The weekdays have gone by, and now it's Sunday again. The cycle of another week begins. One Sunday follows another, and we learn to ask "*What* Sunday is it?" What Sunday in the season? What Sunday in the year? The Lord's Day is not only the foundation of the Christian week, it is also the foundation of the Christian year.

As there is a rapid and continuous rhythm of call and response going on every moment of our worship, a less-rapid rhythm of call and response by which the acts of worship in the Sunday service are arranged, a slower rhythm of night and day, and a still slower rhythm that structures the week around the Lord's Day, so there is a rhythm in the sequence of Lord's Days that gives structure to the Christian year.

The rhythm of the Christian year has its roots in the Bible, took its basic shape in the early church, and has continued to develop over the centuries.

The Easter Cycle

We read in both the Old and New Testaments how the people of ancient Israel observed a variety of yearly festivals which related both to the agriculture which structured their lives and to the events in their history which constituted their story as a people. It was very significant to Jesus and his first disciples that he was crucified at Passover time, when Jews were commemorating how God had delivered their ancestors from slavery in Egypt, brought them safely through the Red Sea, and made them a free people. We, too, these earliest Christians realized, have been delivered by God and are no longer slaves to sin and death. We have been made a free people through the suffering, death, and resurrection of Christ. Referring to the lamb which was sacrificed at Passover, Paul said: "Christ, our paschal [Passover] lamb, has been sacrificed. Let us, therefore, celebrate the festival" (I Corinthians 5:7-8).

And so, although the early Christians celebrated God's saving work in Christ every Sunday, it seemed fitting when Passover time came around each year that there be some sort of great yearly Lord's Day. Christians were observing this *Pascha* (Passover) at least as early as the second century and possibly even in New Testament times.

Its climax was the baptizing of new Christians, followed by Holy Communion which for the first time included these new Christians as members of the Body of Christ. Baptism was seen as being delivered through water into freedom in Christ, like the delivery of Israel through the Red Sea. It was burial and resurrection with Christ (Romans 6:4-5).

There had to be preparation for such a solemn act. Hippolytus, writing in the third century, tells that those to be baptized fasted on Friday and Saturday and then took part in a vigil all Saturday night. Sunday morning at cockcrow, the hour when Christ was said to have risen from the dead, they were baptized beneath the waters and rose with Christ as from the dead.

During the fourth century the *Pascha* was divided into several observances spread over several days. The institution of the Lord's Supper was commemorated on Thursday evening, Jesus' death on Friday, and his resurrection on Saturday night and Sunday morning. These observances became Holy (Maundy) Thursday, Good Friday, and Easter. The word *Easter*, used in English-speaking countries, comes from the Anglo-Saxon *Eastre*, the name of a pagan goddess and her spring festival. Other languages such as French, Spanish, and Italian still use words derived from *Pascha* which make it evident that we are celebrating the Christian Passover. The Great Three Days—sometimes called the *Triduum*—from sunset Holy Thursday through sunset Easter Day are still the climax of the Christian year.

Also in the fourth century the week before Easter began to be observed as Holy Week, beginning with the Sunday we know as Passion (Palm) Sunday, when Jesus' entry into Jerusalem and subsequent passion (suffering) are commemmorated. The early weekdays of Holy Week have always been of less importance than the Great Three Days, and today there is a renewed emphasis on the Great Three Days as a unified Christian Passover.

You may have wondered why Easter falls on a different date each year. Like the Jewish Passover, it is determined by the phases of the moon. Early Christians debated the proper date for the *Pascha* and agreed in the fourth century that it, unlike the Jewish Passover, must always be celebrated on a Sunday so that the weekly and yearly celebrations of Jesus' resurrection reinforce each other. Later in western Europe it came to be observed on the Sunday after the first full moon on or after the first day of spring, which can place Easter as early as March 22 or as late as April 25. This is how Roman Catholics and Protestants still date Easter.

Easter is more than a day. It is a season which the early Christians called the Great Fifty Days, beginning with Easter Day and extending through Pentecost on the fiftieth day (seven Sundays) following. It commemorates the fifty days that began when Jesus rose from the dead and ended when the disciples received the Holy Spirit and the Christian church was born. This season, already well established by the third century, is like a continuous fifty-day Lord's Day. It was seen by the early Christians as being to the year what the Lord's Day was to the week—the prime one-seventh of the time, when we celebrate what God has done through Christ. Easter, then, is a day of the week, a day of the year, and a season of the year. It is not only a commemoration of Jesus' resurrection but a fully trinitarian celebration. Since ancient times it has been celebrated as the season of God's creation and new creation, the season of the risen and ever-present

Christ, and the season of the coming of the Holy Spirit and the gifts and fruits of the Spirit.

The emphasis on the Holy Spirit reaches its climax on the fiftieth and last day of the season, the day of Pentecost, which brings the Easter Season to a glorious close. Pentecost, which in Greek means "fiftieth" (day), was the name Greek-speaking Jews gave to the Jewish Day of First Fruits or Feast of Weeks *(Shabuoth),* the harvest festival commanded in Leviticus 23:16. It was the conclusion of the cycle that began at Passover, and the term *Pentecost* was also used to indicate the whole cycle. The early Christians likewise used the term *Pentecost* to refer not only to the day of Pentecost but also to the Great Fifty Days as a whole.

It has been significant for Christians that it was on the Jewish day of Pentecost that the Christian church was born. Sometime in the first century the day of Pentecost became for Jews not only a harvest festival but also a commemoration of the giving of the Torah (teaching, law) on Mount Sinai. Whether or not this had occurred by the time the account of the Christian day of Pentecost (Acts 2) was written, Christians from early times have drawn the parallel between the giving of the Torah and the giving of the Holy Spirit. Possibly even Paul is relating the two Pentecosts in II Corinthians 3:7-8. As God brought covenant with Israel to fruition on Mount Sinai, so God brought covenant with the disciples of Christ to fruition at Pentecost and gave birth to the Christian church.

The day of Pentecost, at least as early as the second century, was a time when the church baptized candidates who were not ready at Easter. Pentecost has always seemed an appropriate day for baptisms. We read in Acts 2:41 that on the day of Pentecost about three thousand persons were baptized. The day we celebrate the birth of the church is surely a fitting time to celebrate the spiritual birth of a Christian. Christians from ancient times have thought of the gathering in of converts as like a harvest (Matthew 9:37-38, Luke 10:2, John 4:35) and have naturally thought of the Great Fifty Days with its harvest origins in ancient Israel as our great spiritual harvest season.

At first the day of Pentecost was a celebration of Christ's

ascension (Acts 1:1-11) as well as of the coming of the Holy Spirit (Acts 2). By the end of the fourth century, Christians had begun to celebrate Ascension as a separate festival on the fortieth day of the Easter Season, remembering the reference in Acts 1:3 to the forty-day period between Christ's resurrection and ascension. This festival falls on the Thursday following the sixth Sunday of the Easter Season. Many congregations who find it hard to hold a service on Thursday observe the following Sunday as Ascension Sunday.

The Easter Season soon came to be seen as requiring a season of preparation. This season, known as Lent, began in the early church as a period of final preparation and examination for those to be baptized at Easter. They had already undergone a long period of preparation and were now ready for the final "scrutinies," as they were called. The length of this final preparatory period as being forty days was first mentioned in the early fourth century. The forty days came to be seen as comparable to Jesus' forty days in the wilderness, when he fasted and prepared himself for his ministry. By the fifth century Lent was understood as a time of preparation by *all* Christians for the renewal of the whole church at Easter. Fasting, as a means to the spiritual discipline needed by Christians, was an important part of Lent. This made Lent a rather somber and strenuous season. Sometimes the emphasis has been negative—self-denial for its own sake. This is one reason some Christians have reacted against observing Lent. At other times, and increasingly today, the emphasis has been positive—preparation for the Easter renewal of our Christian commitment.

Even in Lent every Lord's Day is a little Easter in which we encounter the risen Christ and celebrate his victory. The fact that it is the Lord's Day is more important than the fact that it is in the season of Lent. For this reason, the six Sundays in Lent are not counted as part of the forty days. Lent thus has a total of forty-six days, beginning with Ash Wednesday (the seventh Wednesday before Easter) and concluding at sunset the day before Easter.

The seasons of Lent and Easter together, from Ash Wednesday through the day of Pentecost, are included in the

Easter Cycle—a great time of renewal each year in which the church and its members are challenged to move "from ashes to fire."

With all this history in mind, look at what happens in your local church during the Easter Cycle.

Partly your congregation will be commemorating key events in the life of Christ—his forty days in the wilderness and subsequent ministry, his entry into Jerusalem and suffering there, his institution of the Holy Communion, his death, his resurrection, his ascension, and the coming of the Holy Spirit.

But this can be merely history except as it is linked with what is happening here and now. During the Easter Cycle persons are probably baptized, or confirmed, or received into your church by transfer or by reaffirmation of their faith. Prior to these ceremonies the candidates are probably instructed as may be necessary in the meaning of Christian faith and church membership. Following these ceremonies is a crucial time for assimilating these new members into the Body. Furthermore, the whole Body needs to be prepared for the "grafting in" of these new members if the process is to "take." Lent is a time when congregations and their members are likely to be challenged, both in worship and in classes and small groups, to commitment and growth in Christian faith and life. A growing number of churches are reviving the ancient Easter Vigil, either Saturday night or at sunrise, with its focus on Christian baptism and renewal.

Churches that in the past have let everything slacken off after Easter Day are rediscovering the joy of the Great Fifty Days. The Sundays of the Easter Season, leading to Ascension and Pentecost, can be jubilant celebrations with the risen Christ in the power of the Holy Spirit. Choirs and other creative persons, if they do not exhaust themselves during Holy Week, can see that music and other arts are at their most glorious during the Great Fifty Days. Classes and groups that begin in Lent can continue until the day of Pentecost.

What does going from ashes to fire mean—what might it mean—in your church?

The Christmas Cycle

The other great high period of the Christian year is the time around Christmas—the Christmas Cycle. Its origins in Christian history are not quite so early as those of the Easter Cycle, nor are they rooted in the festivals of ancient Israel. But so meaningful have Christmas and all that surrounds it become to Christian people that Christmas has joined Easter as one of the two peaks of the Christian year.

The feast of Epiphany is not so well known as Christmas, but it is older and was even more important in early Christian history. It falls on January 6, although in many churches today it is celebrated on the nearest Sunday or on the first Sunday in January. The word *epiphany* means "manifestation." In Christian use it refers particularly to the manifestation of God in Jesus Christ—in his birth and baptism, in various later events in his ministry, and at last in his coming in final victory. The Christian feast of Epiphany probably began in Egypt, at least as early as the late second century.

At first, Epiphany celebrated both the birth and baptism of Christ; but during the fourth century it, like the *Pascha*, was split. Epiphany itself remained on January 6. In the East it remained the celebration of Jesus' baptism, while in western Europe it became the celebration of the visit of the wise men, who represented the manifestation of God to the Gentiles.

The other and newer festival, which in time came to dominate the cycle, was Christmas. The first mention of December 25 as Jesus' birthdate is A.D. 354, and there is evidence that this date may have been observed by Christians in Rome about 336 and in Africa prior to 312. As Christianity became the established religion of the Roman Empire, Christmas served as the replacement for the existing pagan festivities at the winter solstice.

Both Christmas and Epiphany represent, as do developments in the Easter Cycle at the same time, a growing desire on the part of the early Christians to celebrate the anniversaries of specific days in the life of Christ. The Bible says nothing to indicate the day of the year on which Jesus was either born or baptized, and it is possible that the dates of January 6 and December 25 may have originated in winter solstice celebrations according to the ancient Egyptian and Julian (Roman) calendars, respectively. At any rate, the theme of light conquering darkness has always been prominent in both of these Christian festivals.

Christmas, like Easter, became not only a day but a season celebrating the manifestation of God in Jesus Christ. Both the day and the season begin at sunset Christmas Eve, but the exact length of the season has varied from one tradition and denomination to another. "The Twelve Days of Christmas," celebrated by the song, take the season through January 5 (Twelfth Night) but do not include Epiphany. Today, however, Christian churches increasingly extend the Christmas Season through Epiphany to recover a unified Christmas-Epiphany season, which like the Easter-Pentecost season includes two great days and the time between.

In recent years both Catholic and Protestant churches have been recovering the old emphasis on the baptism of Christ at Epiphany by celebrating the Sunday after January 6 as the Baptism of the Lord while keeping Epiphany itself as the commemoration of the visit of the wise men.

As early as the late fourth century, Christians saw that Christmas-Epiphany needed a preparatory season comparable to what Lent was becoming in the Easter Cycle. This eventually became Advent as we know it, which begins on the fourth Sunday before Christmas and continues to sunset Christmas Eve. While penitence and spiritual discipline have sometimes been emphasized in Advent, as in Lent, the dominant note of the season has been hope and expectancy. The word *advent* means "coming." In Advent the church has celebrated its hope and expectancy in the comings of Christ—past, present, and future. We identify with those in ancient Israel who looked for the coming of the Messiah, and we look forward ourselves to the yearly celebration of Christ's birth and manifestation. We look for the coming of Christ here and now through the power of the Holy Spirit. We look forward to Christ's coming in final victory.

How do you and your local church celebrate the Christmas Cycle?

In most churches Christmas is almost, but not quite, as high a point in the Christian year as Easter. Music and other arts have an especially large part in our worship during Advent and Christmas. The main emphasis is usually upon Sunday services, but festive services are commonly held on Christmas Eve and sometimes on Christmas Day as well.

There is a strong tendency for the Sundays after Christmas to be experienced as a letdown and for Advent to become the Christmas Season rather than the season preparatory to the Christmas Season. In many Protestant churches, particularly those which do not hold Christmas Eve or Christmas Day services, the high point of the Christmas Cycle is "Christmas Sunday" on the Fourth Sunday of Advent, the Sunday before Christmas.

There has been a strong movement in recent years to restore Advent as a preparatory season. Advent candles are lit, reminding us that Christmas is still to come. Advent hymns are increasingly sung, especially during the earlier Sundays of Advent. If Christmas carols cannot be held back until Christmas Eve, they may at least be saved until the latter Sundays of Advent.

But the Christmas Cycle is by no means confined to churches. It is probably the biggest celebration of the year in most American homes and in the American society at large.

What is celebrated in our society at large as the Christmas season is a complex mixture of the Christian and the secular—Jesus' birthday and a midwinter festival. One need not be a Christian to dream of a white Christmas, sing of sleigh bells, set up a Christmas tree, exchange gifts and cards, or go to Christmas parties; but as Christians we can do all these things in the spirit of the Christ whose birth we celebrate. The secular Christmas season begins well before Advent, and in fact a very large part of our preparation for Christmas consists of activities like shopping and card- and letter-sending. These preparations can be as much or as little in the spirit of Christ as we choose to make them.

For most Christians in America, the Christmas Cycle is even more a home celebration than a church celebration. Advent and Christmas mean shopping, decorating Christmas trees, preparing and eating Christmas foods, family reunions, gift-giving rituals, reading or telling Christmas stories, and watching Christmas television specials. Those Protestant churches that have no Christmas Eve or Christmas Day services commonly defend this practice by saying that Christmas should be observed by families at home. When Christmas Day falls on a Sunday, attendance suffers because so many families choose to spend Christmas morning at home with their customary family ceremonies rather than attending church services.

Indeed, a major reason for the increase in recent years of Protestant Christmas Eve and Christmas Day services appears to be the growing number of persons who are not part of traditional nuclear families or who are unable to be with their families at Christmas, and who make church services their family Christmas celebrations.

Churches have become increasingly sensitive to the needs of the many persons for whom Christmas is a lonely time or for whom the season brings demands and strains that are hard to cope with. Ways are being found that enable persons to support each other at difficult times. Many persons invite others who cannot be with their families or have no families to join them for Christmas Eve or Christmas morning or Christmas dinner.

Where does this whole celebration of the Christmas Cycle lead so far as Christian commitment is concerned?

Many churches have an observance around New Year's or early in January for the renewal of our Christian covenant. It may be a Watchnight service. It may be the January communion service. It may be the Sunday after Epiphany—the Baptism of the Lord—which is often observed as Covenant Sunday. Such a covenant service is an appropriate time for baptisms and for members of the whole congregation to renew their Christian covenant. It is a way of adapting the ancient tradition of Epiphany to modern America and bringing the Christmas Cycle to a fitting conclusion.

Through the Year

So far we have dealt with the high seasons of the Christian year, which have their origins in the first four centuries of

Christian history and which must be understood if we are to see the Christian year as a whole.

The profile of the Christian year has not only peaks and high plateaus but also plains and valleys. The parts of the Christian year that are not in the Christmas or Easter cycles are sometimes called ordinary time. We should not consider the word *ordinary* as a put-down of these times in the year. Rather, it calls attention to the fact that the year is not one "high" after another but has a profile in which the high seasons are what they are because there are other seasons where there is more of a steady, week-in, week-out feel to worship.

The Christian year begins on the First Sunday of Advent, and for the first few weeks that constitute the Christmas Cycle we have a very intense sense of what season it is in the Christian year.

Then comes the Season after Epiphany, which lasts until Lent begins—sometime between February 4 and March 10. Although the lectionary readings echo Epiphany by dealing with various epiphanies of Christ, we are not really conscious of what season it is in the Christian year. Those of us who live in the north temperate zone of the earth are much more conscious of the fact that it is winter. Whether or not the weather is severe enough to reduce church attendance, this time tends to feel like a valley in the profile of the year—both in and out of church. However, this season is framed by two important observances. The First Sunday after Epiphany, as we have seen, is the Baptism of the Lord. The Last Sunday after Epiphany is Transfiguration Sunday in many Protestant denominations and commemorates the Transfiguration of Jesus (Matthew 17:1-9, Mark 9:2-10, Luke 9:28-36, II Peter 1:17-18).

Then in the Easter Cycle, Christians tend again to be very conscious of what season it is in the Christian year.

The whole second half of the Christian year is the Season after Pentecost, which lasts from the day after Pentecost—sometime in May or June—until Advent begins the Christian year again. This season, or parts of it, has been called by various names such as Trinity, Pentecost, Whitsuntide, and

Kingdomtide; but the fact is that we are not really conscious of its being a liturgical season.

In the north temperate zone of the earth, the weather and the rhythms of secular life make us conscious of the fact that it is summer and then fall. Summer may mean a slump, complete with choir vacation and guest preachers; or in recreational areas it may be the peak season with many visitors. "The busy fall season" is likely to feel like the beginning of the church year as congregations launch into their fall programs.

Beginning with the First Sunday after Pentecost, which is Trinity Sunday, this time is full of special days and occasions. In the summer there are camps and conferences, outdoor services, and revival meetings. In the fall there is a host of days during which various church causes are promoted. This half of the year has more than its share of the major civil holidays in the United States; and if church attendance hits lows on Memorial Day, Fourth of July, and Labor Day weekends it is because so many of us are enjoying the time away from home with family and friends.

On the other hand, the steady continuity of preaching that goes through books of the Bible, as the lectionary provides for in this half of the year, and the planning of worship around these Scriptures Sunday by Sunday may give a congregation more spiritual nurture than a constant search for some special emphasis each Sunday.

By November we are on an upward slope toward another high season, and these last few weeks of the Christian year are also a bridge to Advent and the new Christian year. Choirs are rehearsing Advent and Christmas music; Christmas programs are in preparation; and the world outside the church is already launching the Christmas season. A growing number of congregations celebrate All Saints' on the first day or the first Sunday of November, remembering the great parade of Christians through the ages who constitute the communion of saints. In congregations that follow the lectionary, the November readings center on the kingship of Christ and lead up to the last Sunday of the Christian year—the festival of Christ the King—and then to the celebration of our King's advent.

Thanksgiving in the United States, the fourth Thursday in November, is perhaps the one occasion in the year that most reflects our civil religion. It can be celebrated by Christians, Jews, and persons of other religions and is sometimes celebrated by interreligious services. It is also an important day for home religious rituals, often centering on Thanksgiving dinner and family reunions. Football games provide secular ritual. Churches may have their own or union services on Thanksgiving Day, Eve, or Sunday, at which thanks are given for the fruits of the earth, our heritage as an American people, or all God's blessings.

Through the Christian year we are reminded of the day and season by bulletins and hymn boards, Scriptures and sermons, hymns and anthems, prayers and acts of praise.

But it is by visuals that days and seasons may most immediately be announced—lilies at Easter and poinsettias at Christmas, chancel paraments and clergy stoles, banners and other hangings. While there is no universally accepted color code for the Christian year, there are some associations of colors with days and seasons which are in fairly general use in many American denominations.

White and gold are considered joyous and festive colors and are commonly used during the Christmas and Easter seasons and on other high days such as All Saints'.

Purple suggests both royalty and penitence and is commonly used during Advent and Lent. Blue, the color of hope and of Mary the mother of Jesus, is also sometimes used during Advent.

Red as the color of blood is often used during Holy Week and to commemorate martyrs. As the color of fire it is generally used on the day of Pentecost and may be used whenever the work of the Holy Spirit is emphasized.

Green as the color of growth and hope is used after Epiphany and after Pentecost. During these periods of ordinary time, white and red are often used on particular days as appropriate.

However we celebrate the changing days and seasons of the year, we are sanctifying the time and letting it teach us the things of God.

ELEVEN

Initiation and Passages

The Great Cycles and Beyond

The seasons recur year after year, but all years are not the same—just as the days and seasons of the year, the days of the week, the hours of the day, and the moments within an hour or within a worship service are not the same. Whenever we celebrate birthdays or anniversaries of any sort we answer the question, "What year is it?" The fact that we number our years A.D.—an abbreviation for *anno Domini*, which is Latin for "in the year of the Lord"—reminds us that it has been almost two thousand years since the birth of Christ. At New Year's we may celebrate in our worship that we are entering a new and different "year of the Lord."

Anniversary services are a significant part of the worship of most churches. Congregations and entire denominations celebrate their fiftieth, hundredth, or two-hundredth anniversaries with appropriate services. Sometimes the celebration recalls an important episode in a congregation's history such as the erection of its present building; sometimes it commemorates a crucial event in a denomination's history or in the life of its founder. Such celebrations tell us that the cycles of time include even such great cycles as centuries. How will our second century compare with our first, or our third with our second?

Beyond even these great cycles of time, however, there are passages in the life of a church or a person that will never recur. Once the passage is made, not only will that church or that person never be the same again, the passage itself cannot be repeated.

Baptism

In Christian worship the most basic of these rites of passage, as they are called, is baptism. Through baptism one is initiated not only into a congregation but also into the universal church, "grafted" as a new member into the Body of Christ, marked and identified as a Christian disciple. When speaking of baptism, many persons in recent years have used the term *Christian initiation.*

Baptism is as much a rite of passage for the church as it is for the person baptized. When a new member is joined to the Body of Christ neither the member nor the Body will ever be the same again. The church commits itself to nurture its new member through its worship, through church school classes and other nurturing groups, through pastoral care, and through the ongoing love and concern of the other members—regardless of whether the one being baptized is an infant or a mature adult. One or more sponsors, elder brothers and sisters in Christ, may agree to take special responsibilities for guiding and nurturing the one baptized. In the case of the baptized child this responsibility is especially crucial and is normally assigned to the parent(s), although there may be other sponsors (godparents) as well. If the baptized person later becomes part of another congregation, that congregation recognizes the person as a baptized member of the universal church and assumes the appropriate nurturing responsibilities toward that person. Baptism is, therefore, an act of worship where both the congregation and the candidate—or the parent(s) or sponsor(s)—make solemn promises and accept solemn responsibilities.

Baptism has been one of the basics of Christian worship since New Testament times. Jesus was baptized as the opening act of his public ministry (Matthew 3:13-17, Mark 1:9-11, Luke 3:21-22). We read in Matthew 28:19 that after his resurrection Jesus commanded the disciples to "make disciples of all nations, baptizing them in the name of the Father and of the Son and of the Holy Spirit." After Peter preached on the day of Pentecost, the day the church came into being, "those who received his word were baptized, and there were added that day about three thousand souls" (Acts 2:41).

Baptism itself is a washing with water, and like Holy Communion it is a basic human act through which God acts in our lives. Like Holy Communion, it is commonly called a sacrament and an ordinance, and it is a mystery through which we participate in the mystery of the gospel. It means more than any explanation can tell us, and the many New Testament references to baptism describe its meanings through a variety of images. Each image shows one or more facets of baptism, but no one image shows us the whole meaning. We are baptized into union with Christ—into death, burial, and resurrection with Christ (Romans 6:3-5, Colossians 2:12). We are incorporated by baptism into one body, the church, in which we have put on Christ like a garment and are all one in Christ (I Corinthians 12:13, Galatians 3:27-28). Baptism signifies being born anew of water and the Spirit (John 3:3-5, Titus 3:5). The cleansing action of water in baptism represents the forgiveness of sin (Acts 2:38 and 22:16, I Corinthians 6:11, Hebrews 10:22, I Peter 3:21). Baptism represents the receiving of the Holy Spirit (Matthew 3:16, Mark 1:9-10, Luke 3:21-22, Acts 2:38 and 19:1-7).

All these biblical images make it clear that baptism is a sign of what God does for us in Christ. God has taken the initiative in making covenant with us, and whatever we do in faith is always in response to what God has already done for us. The response of faith, however, is essential to making God's gifts effective in our lives.

It is unfortunate that baptism, which makes us one in Christ, has so often been the occasion of estrangement among Christians because of differing interpretations, each of which can claim support from one or more of the above images.

Exactly how should persons be baptized? Should they be totally immersed in the water, as suggested by the image of burial and resurrection with Christ? Should the water be poured or sprinkled on their heads, as suggested by the image of pouring out the Holy Spirit? Does immersion in flowing water suggest more of these images than immersion in still water? Perhaps it is best that baptism take place in a variety of such modes, so as to bring out the different facets of its rich imagery. Many churches today give candidates for baptism, or their parents, a choice of modes and are glad that some persons choose one mode and others another mode.

A still deeper division among Christians concerns whether or not infants may be baptized.

Many Christians believe that infants cannot make the essential response of faith to what God has done for them, and that baptism should therefore be delayed until the candidate is able to make a public profession of faith. They also point out that nowhere in the New Testament is it clearly stated that an infant was baptized.

Most Christians, however, believe that an infant who is part of a Christian household may be baptized. They point out that God's covenant with ancient Israel treated the family as a unit and that if God's new covenant through Christ had been different at this point the New Testament writers would surely have felt it necessary to make the difference clear—which they did not. On the contrary, Peter on the day of Pentecost clearly reinforces treating the family as a unit by saying: "Repent, and be baptized. . . . For the promise is to you and to your children" (Acts 2:38-39). Furthermore, when the head of a household made a profession of faith, the whole household was baptized (Acts 16:15, 16:33, and 18:8; I Corinthians 1:16). We may assume that some of these households contained children too young to make a public profession of faith. If there is no clear statement in the New Testament that an infant was baptized, neither is there a clear statement that anyone born and raised in a Christian family made a profession of faith sometime in the course of growing up and was then baptized. Many believe that little children have their own form of faith, appropriate to their level of development if not yet expressed in thoughts and words; and Jesus' statement in Mark 10:13-16 is often quoted in this connection.

Regardless of the age of the person being baptized, we may say that the response of faith to what God has done is given by the whole congregation or even the whole universal church, to which total response the candidates and their parents or sponsors contribute what they can at their particular level of mental and spiritual development. Even candidates making their own professions of faith are in most cases "babes in Christ." No one can say, "My personal faith is good enough." We all can say, *"God's* grace—*God's* undeserved love—*is* good enough."

What happens in a service when there are baptisms?

Sometimes the rite of baptism is a fairly incidental part of a Sunday service, the rest of which has little or nothing to do with baptism, but increasingly churches are holding baptisms on occasions in the Christian year when the baptisms can be the focus of the service. Any Sunday during the Great Fifty Days lends itself to baptisms, especially Easter Day and the day of Pentecost. Where the ancient Easter Vigil has been revived, baptism finds what is perhaps its ideal setting. The Baptism of the Lord (Covenant Sunday) in January and All Saints' in November are also appropriate occasions.

How much preparation should there be for baptism?

The early church took such preparation very seriously. Candidates were often prepared for three years or more before baptism. We have seen that Lent originated as the time when candidates for baptism underwent their final "scrutinies" and that Lent became also a time of renewal for the whole church. Persons were given additional instruction and nurture following baptism.

If a new member is to be grafted into the Body of Christ, then it is important both that the new member be suitable and prepared for the grafting and that the Body also be prepared to accept and not reject the new member. The Easter Cycle is a particularly appropriate time for this process. If your church has a tradition of annual revival meetings or special evangelistic services at some other time of year, this may serve a similar purpose. In any case, the candidate for baptism or the parent(s) of a child to be baptized should be carefully prepared for such an important step. The congregation should not take it for granted that it can assimilate the new member but should be carefully prepared for this step, remembering that even the addition of a new baby imposes a heavy responsibility on the nurturing congregation.

The rite of baptism itself consists of several acts.

There is the renunciation of evil and the profession of faith, spoken by the candidate or the candidate's parents but also supported by the congregation as a whole and any other individual sponsors. These are sometimes called the vows.

Often the minister then gives thanks over the water, very much as the minister at Holy Communion gives thanks over the bread and wine, recalling what God has done for us in Christ, invoking the action of the Holy Spirit, and praying for those being baptized.

Then water is applied in the name of the Trinity. Since water has great sign value, it should be used conspicuously. There is a growing trend among those who baptize by pouring or sprinkling to use enough water that it can be seen and perhaps even heard as it is used.

In the early church (Acts 8:14-17) and increasingly today the minister and perhaps others lay hands upon the head of the person who has just been baptized, and the minister invokes the Holy Spirit.

Sometimes the ancient practice of anointing (christening) with oil is also followed. The word *Christ* means "the anointed one," and anointing identifies the person with Christ.

Finally, it is fitting and traditional that those just baptized join the rest of the congregation in Holy Communion as the completion of their Christian initiation.

Baptism is part of a lifelong process, as the very term *initiation* implies. What baptism signifies with respect to union with Christ, incorporation into Christ's Body, spiritual rebirth, forgiveness of sin, and receiving of the Holy Spirit does not happen all at once, but over the course of a lifetime. Whether the candidate is a baby or an adult, baptism looks backward to the grace of God which anticipated the candidate's birth and has been present from the beginning of life, and it looks forward to all that God will do in the rest of that person's life and eternally. The repentance and faith professed at baptism are part of an ongoing and developing life of repentance and faith, both for the church and for the individual member. The forgiveness of sin which baptism signifies is not simply forgiveness for sins committed previously but a lifelong process of forgiveness for the sin of a lifetime. Having been baptized in and of itself never entitles anyone to say, "Now I'm saved and am going to heaven." Nor would we ever say of anyone just because that person has not been baptized that she or he is not saved.

In the course of this lifelong process there are other rites of passage which are part of our worship and which build upon baptism. To these we now turn.

Other Professions and Reaffirmations

It is an essential and crucial step in Christian development when persons first profess for themselves the Christian faith. Churches carefully nurture their children and youth toward this step in church school classes and commonly also in special classes taught by the pastor or some other qualified person. While there is great variation in the age at which persons take this step, depending both on the expectations of the congregation and community and also on the personal readiness of the individual, churches commonly find that most of those under their nurture are ready to profess their faith sometime in later childhood or in their early teens. If they have not already been baptized, they may make this profession at their baptism. If they are already baptized, the church provides another rite at which they can publicly profess their faith in the presence of the congregation. This rite goes by various names, the most common of which is confirmation.

The term *confirmation* has three important meanings: (1) Candidates confirm their personal commitment by accepting and renewing for themselves the vows made at baptism. (2) God reconfirms the covenant in Christ to those who were too young to understand it when they were baptized. (3) The congregation confirms these persons in their relationship to the family of Christ and in the ministries to which all Christians are commissioned by baptism.

This rite always includes the candidates' profession of faith and often also includes the laying of hands upon the candidates' heads with the invocation of the Holy Spirit. Various other ceremonies and celebrations may be included.

There are other occasions when persons profess their faith in a new way. This can happen at any stage in a person's life, and the character of this profession will vary with the person's level of faith development. It can represent a deepening of a commitment that was already present or the recovery of a commitment that had for a time been lost or a new commitment. It may follow an experience which the person can tell about. Sometimes the person's life has been clearly, even radically, changed. At other times there seems to have been a steady growth toward the new stage of faith which the person now professes.

Churches often provide persons with the opportunity to tell about an experience or to profess a new or deepened faith and commitment. This may be done during congregational worship or in some more informal and intimate setting.

Such witnessing and professing can be an important step for the church as well as for the individual. This new faith and commitment can bring growth and power to the whole church. It may also require of the church some difficult soul-searching and patient nurture. Persons who have grown up in a congregation or participated actively in its life may say of their previous professions of faith, "I didn't know what I was doing." They may ask accusingly, "Why didn't you ever teach me this?" They may use words or a style of talking or practices which are unfamiliar or unacceptable to others in the congregation. A student home from college or studying for the ministry may denounce the congregation for its real or imagined shortcomings. By bearing with such witnessing and being patient with persons who are struggling to incorporate new experiences into their ongoing lives and relationships, a congregation can grow in Christ while nurturing the growth of these persons.

Sometimes there is need for an act of reconciliation. Someone who has been estranged from the church, perhaps after a bad incident, faces the people and makes or receives needed apologies. Someone may want and need to say, "I don't know how you can have been so patient with me." Persons witnessing to a new Christian experience found outside the four walls of their church may feel estranged as they wonder, "How can I tell the folks back at my home church what has happened to me?" For a congregation to rise to such an occasion and affirm such persons may be a rite of passage for everyone concerned.

Sometimes events in the life of a congregation, its community, or the nation make a corporate service of repentance or reconciliation appropriate.

Healing services are held in many churches, often with Holy Communion. What happens at these may be anything from radically life-changing to quietly supportive, depending on the moving of the Spirit. Through such services persons and congregations can grow in Christ.

There are passages in the history of a congregation that give opportunity for affirming in some new way its faith and ministry as a church. A congregation is organized and holds its first worship service. Ground is broken, or a foundation stone is laid, for a new building. A church building is opened for worship, or its indebtedness is paid off. New furnishings or musical instruments or hymnals or robes are put into use. A final service is held in an old building that is to be razed or given over to other use. A congregation is disbanded, or two or more congregations are merged. A minister is installed or retires or leaves. Other church staff, boards and committees, choirs and instrumentalists, church school workers, ushers, and all manner of volunteers may be installed or recognized and thanked. On such occasions rites of blessing and consecration are held.

Ordinations and Consecrations

It is a very special rite of passage when one or more persons are ordained or consecrated to particular lifetime ministries within the general ministry of all Christians.

Some denominations have *bishops*, a term translated from a New Testament word meaning "overseer" (Philippians 1:1, I Timothy 3:1-7, Titus 1:7-9). Most denominations have *presbyters*, a frequently used New Testament term which Christians have commonly translated either "elder" or "priest." Many denominations have *deacons,* a New Testament term meaning "servant" or "attendant" (Romans 16:1, Philippians 1:1, I Timothy 3:8-13, and perhaps Acts 6:1-7). In recent years persons have also been consecrated to other ministries such as Christian education or church music. Such ordinations and consecrations differ widely from one denomination to another, but they normally take place in the context of a worship service and are closely related to the basic structures of worship which we have already discussed.

Baptism is the basic ordination and consecration to the work of Christian ministry, and all further ordinations and consecrations build upon the foundation of baptism. Christ's great commission (Matthew 28:19-20) and the enabling power of the Holy Spirit (Acts 1 and 2) were not restricted to a group of professionals but were given to all Christians. The whole Letter to the Hebrews makes it clear that Christ alone is our high priest, and the First Letter of Peter tells baptized Christians that they are a priesthood (2:5 and 9). Within this priesthood, or ministry, "there are varieties of gifts, but the same Spirit; and there are varieties of service, but the same Lord" (I Corinthians 12:4-5). "[Christ's] gifts were that some should be apostles, some prophets, some evangelists, some pastors and teachers, to equip the saints for the work of ministry, for building up the body of Christ" (Ephesians 4:11-12). "The saints" in New Testament usage refers to the whole body of Christians, and it is the function of persons such as pastors and teachers to use their special gifts and calling to equip the whole body for the work of ministry.

Ordination and consecration services are commonly services of the Word and traditionally also Holy Communion. A charge based upon Scripture is given to the candidate(s) and to those among whom the candidate(s) will be serving. The act of ordination or consecration commonly has as its visible sign the laying on of hands, with the invocation of the Holy Spirit. This recalls baptism and perhaps confirmation, and it signifies that it is not only the church but, ultimately, God who ordains. There may be other acts such as the giving of a Bible, chalice, or stole; but these are secondary to the laying on of hands with prayer. When Holy Communion concludes the service, the newly ordained or consecrated may take an appropriate role in addition to receiving communion.

Christian Marriage

Marriage is a broadly human institution that among Christians may be solemnized—blessed or consecrated—in a service of Christian worship. While the marriages of early Christians were sometimes blessed during worship, it is only gradually over the centuries that this practice has come to be expected, and there is wide variation in practice to this day.

In the United States ordained clergy as well as certain civil magistrates are authorized to be agents of the state in officiating at legal marriages. Christians may choose to be married before a civil magistrate instead of a Christian minister, and a Christian minister may choose to officiate at the marriage of non-Christians if permitted by the church to do so. When Christians marry before a Christian minister it is not always done in a church sanctuary or chapel; and even when it is, it is not always done in a service of worship. Often in marriages acts of worship such as prayers are mixed with secular music and other symbolism not usually associated with worship.

Nevertheless, many if not most Christians marry in a service of worship. This may be simply a blessing, often at the Lord's table, following the exchange of vows and declaration by the minister that the couple are now husband and wife. It may also involve replacing secular processional and recessional music with Christian hymns and having vocalists sing music appropriate to Christian worship. For a growing number of couples it includes a Service of the Word, the marriage rite itself, and Holy Communion. This is usually done as a separate service, but some couples are married during a regular Sunday service of their local congregation.

Marriage is transformed for Christians when it is based upon the foundation of baptism. As baptism initiates a new member into the Body of Christ and a covenant relationship with God through Christ, so Christian marriage can be seen as uniting two persons as one flesh (Mark 10:8, Ephesians

5:28-31) in a marriage covenant modeled after our covenant relationship with Christ (I Corinthians 11:2, Ephesians 5:21-33, Revelation 21:2).

Holy Communion on this occasion means not only that the couple begin their marriage by being joined in the supreme act of Christian worship, the acting out of our union with Christ, but also that they do this as part of the wider communion of saints, the Body of Christ. For this reason it is appropriate that not only the couple but others be invited to receive communion, even though some for various reasons may choose not to do so.

At any service of Christian marriage, persons present may be reminded of their own marriage covenants and may see these as being reaffirmed by their participation in the marriage of another couple. Couples may also in a service of worship publicly celebrate their wedding anniversary, reaffirm their marriage covenant, or (if they were married in a civil ceremony) affirm their existing marriage for the first time in the covenantal context of Christian worship.

Christian Funerals and Memorial Services

The final passage in life is death. From time immemorial human beings have expressed themselves in ritual when someone dies.

When Christians die their families and friends almost always request some kind of funeral or memorial service that is an act of Christian worship. This is usually conducted by a Christian minister, although occasionally laypersons conduct funerals or memorial services, and secular organizations often conduct rites before or after the service. The traditional funeral is a rite conducted in the presence of the body of the deceased, after which the body is committed to its final resting place, usually burial in the earth. A memorial service is conducted in the absence of the body, either instead of or in addition to a funeral.

Where the funeral or memorial service is a Christian service of worship, it is traditionally based upon the foundation of baptism. It includes a Service of the Word, and sometimes Holy Communion.

The Christian gospel is a message of death and resurrection—Christ's and ours. Christ spoke of his own death, burial, and resurrection as a baptism (Mark 10:38-39, Luke 12:50) in which his disciples were to share, and Paul tells us that in baptism we are buried and raised with Christ (Romans 6:4, Colossians 2:12). Death no longer has dominion over Christ, and if we have died with Christ we believe we shall also live with him (Romans 6:8-9). For the Christian, "to live is Christ, and to die is gain" (Philippians 1:21). Committal of the deceased to God and the body to its final resting place recalls the act of baptism and derives its Christian meaning from God's baptismal covenant with us.

Traditionally the committal is preceded—or occasionally in modern practice followed—by a Service of the Word. A Christian memorial service is usually a Service of the Word. Scripture is read, usually interspersed with prayer and praise. There is commonly preaching that includes both the message from Scripture and personal reference to the deceased. It is fitting that the funeral or memorial service of a Christian be held in the church, but it is often held in a funeral home or special chapel, or in the home of the deceased.

The character of funerals and memorial services varies with the circumstances of the deceased and the mourners but is typically a mixture of honest mourning and Christian affirmation. We acknowledge the reality of death, the pain of our loss, and the inevitability of our own death. We give thanks for the life that was lived and shared with us. We give praise that the one we have loved is eternally safe in God's love, which is also our own hope and security. We worship in the awareness that our gathering includes, invisibly, the whole communion of saints—that in Christ the circle is unbroken.

Holy Communion so wonderfully signifies all of this that it is most appropriate at Christian funerals and memorial services. Sometimes the funeral or memorial service itself is a full Service of the Word and Holy Communion. Sometimes the minister makes Holy Communion the focus of a call upon the family shortly after the funeral. The common meal in which family and perhaps friends so often join on the day of the funeral may have some of this same significance, and to make this evident it is possible to have Holy Communion under the minister's leadership before such a meal.

The Ultimate Vision

Beyond the cycles of time and the passages of human life is the endless circle of eternity. The earthly lifetime of an individual comes to an end one day, but the gift of God is eternal life in Christ. Congregations and denominations, communities and nations also come one day to their end; but the communion of saints is eternal in God's love. The New Testament speaks repeatedly of "the ages" (eons)—"this age," "the close of the age," and "the age to come," but tells us that the immortal God is "King of the ages." The Christ who will come in final victory at the end of the age will bring all who are in Christ into the glory of that victory. We are given the vision of a new heaven and a new earth, after the first heaven and the first earth have passed away. We are told that there will be no temple there, for even our churches and our services of worship will have had their time and ceased to be, in the presence of the God who will be "everything to every one."

Meanwhile, we have "the assurance of things hoped for, the conviction of things not seen." Every morning when we rise from sleep to a new day's life, every Lord's Day when we gather and the rhythm of call and response leads to the consummation of Holy Communion, when in the cycle of the seasons we pass through Good Friday and keep the feast of Easter, and when we celebrate death and resurrection in the passages of life we anticipate the consummation of all things—the ultimate communion. And we know that all shall be well.

For Further Reading

Jones, Cheslyn; Geoffrey Wainwright; and Edward Yarnold. *The Study of Liturgy.* New York: Oxford University Press, 1978. A comprehensive study of Christian worship.

Stookey, Laurence Hull. *Baptism: Christ's Act in the Church.* Nashville: Abingdon Press, 1982. A comprehensive study of baptism.

White, James F. *Introduction to Christian Worship.* Nashville: Abingdon Press, 1980. A comprehensive introduction to Christian worship.

———. *Sacraments as God's Self Giving.* Nashville: Abingdon Press, 1983. A comprehensive study of the meanings of baptism and Holy Communion.

Willimon, William H. *Remember Who You Are.* Nashville: The Upper Room, 1980. A popular study of baptism.

———. *Sunday Dinner.* Nashville: The Upper Room, 1981. A popular study of Holy Communion.

———. *Word, Water, Wine and Bread.* Valley Forge, Penn.: Judson Press, 1980. A popular history of Christian worship.